Other Books by Val Dumond

NONFICTION
The Anarchist's Guide to Grammar
Grammar For Grownups
Elements of Nonsexist Usage
Just Words — The Us and Them Thing
*SHEIT — A No-nonsense Guidebook
To Writing and Using Nonsexist Language*
Doin' the Puyallup
Steilacoom's Church
Olympia Coloring Book

FICTION
Sugar, Spice, and Stone
Ahlam's Stories
*How We Fought World War II
At William T. Sherman Elementary School*
Mush On and Smile (a novel)

ANTHOLOGY
The Sun Never Rises
Dream Makers

This book is dedicated to
Originals everywhere

*The **painter** paints in silence.*
Their work is silent. Their expression and interpretation are silent.

***Musicians** create audible art;*
They express their art with sound, aloud. Listeners interpret in silence.

***Writers** write with inner voices to produce audible words.*
Readers interpret with their inner ears to hear the inner voices.
— Charles Kuralt

Are You Singing Your Song?
(... in a world gone mad)

INTRODUCTION

*There is in each human being an instinct
to create something that is yours,
whether a work of art to share
or a pleasure to enjoy creating.
Are you singing your song?*
—Val Dumond

You were ten years old; you sang all day long,

or

You were ten years old; you kept a journal or diary,

or

You were ten years old; you drew pictures and doodles,

or

You were ten years old; you were fascinated with ants... cars... playing house... dinosaurs... water... bubbles... wood... birds... butterflies... words...

You made believe you were a pilot and "flew planes" all day from the top of the neighbor's tree. You couldn't pass an animal in pain, so you carried a first-aid kit with you. You dreamed up word puzzles to stump your mom. You pleased your dad with what you cooked for supper. You caught the ball and ran sixty yards for the winning touchdown.

Ah, the dreams of a 10-year-old!

The fascination with the power of imagination is widespread, everything from "I coulda been a contender" to "I wanna be a rock star".

Dreams are endless. But *your* dreams may not be. You may be holding onto a very specific dream left over from those days when you were ten, when you sat in the shade and imagined.

Then, around sixteen or eighteen, came reality. Where are you going to college? Why don't you get a job? Are you going to get married? How will you support yourself (a spouse, children)? What are you going to do with your life? Singing — drawing, writing, acting, inventing, cooking (pick one or choose your own) — won't support you. You need a real job! Oh, you can dream, but you need a backup job — "in case it doesn't work out." (Copied from the *Parent's Handbook In My Head.*)

So many of us, perhaps too many of us, put away our ten-year-old fantasies to molder in the background. Too many of us opt for "earning a living" rather than "enjoying living". After all, isn't that the practical way? Conforming?

Music tells us much about ourselves, which is why I chose the title for this book. The idea of conforming to expectations of others was the message in Malvina Reynolds' 1962 hit song, "Little Boxes", where she satirized the "ticky-tacky little boxes" (houses that looked alike) and the people who lived in them. It became a theme song for the Flower Children of the 1960s.

Until years later, when these people we call "baby boomers" asked, "Why didn't I follow my dream?" Dreams are what make us human, whether we paint glorious pictures, produce emotional music, find the beauty in butterflies, prepare sumptuous meals, or write words in a notebook.

Okay, I don't sing like Renée Fleming or Ella Fitzgerald, but I sing — for myself, for the joy of it. Nor do I write songs (it's hard enough to play the written music of others on a piano). But oh, do I love to listen to good music.

"Are you singing your song?" is a metaphor for doing your thing, being creative in your own way, doing the things that make you happy as opposed to the things that other people want you to do.

Writing words in a notebook is me singing my song. I began to hear the words "I used to…" or "I always thought I'd be a…" or "I'd forgotten how that felt when I…" or "Someday I'm going to…" and I paid attention. What I discovered was people expressing their creative bent, and I began to take notes. I wrote down what they said. I present some of my notes here — for you to ponder.

As I wrote, I discovered my own creative instinct was wider than I had ever admitted. For years I told myself, *"Oh, I don't draw; I'm a word person. I don't see pictures. I could never make anything grow. I wish I could cook like Julia Child."* When I took a closer look, I realized that I *do* write, draw ideas and pictures; I grow herbs, cook gourmet meals, knit and crochet; and I draw on memories, fool around with piano keys, and muse at the stars. I *am* actually singing my song.

For many years, I secretly asked myself, "How can a left-brain grammar guru learn to let down her hair and turn into an exciting right-brain, wild, daring person? Why can't I do the thing I love the most — write?" I had to find out how others did it. What resulted is this book, which I consider a dazzling collection of quotations from creative people, mostly well-known authors, artists, and musicians, past and present, as well as lots of other folks I call "Originals". You probably never heard of some of them, such as the bubbleologist, the knife maker, the plumbing manufacturer, the seltzer bottler, and the clown — but oh, they are Originals, living their dreams – their way.

Originals are creative people who have discovered their dreams and are living them. You'll find creative artists talking candidly about what they did as ten-year-olds, how they found inspiration, where they pick up ideas, how they view their gifts/talents/skills.

What are your creative instincts? What is your song? Perhaps you can discover your song among the words of the Originals quoted here.

You may also notice the ages of these Originals, which seems to emphasize the belief that age brings wisdom — and originality — and the courage to live your dream. I included the few younger potential Originals for contrast.

As I collected, one notebook turned into two, then many more. I pored over the comments to learn the secrets of people who seemed to be having such a good time with their lives. Until one day, I took out my computer, pulled out the notes, and began to record them.

Originals come in all ages, all economic levels, all sizes, shapes, and colors, to share their secrets and brief insights into what makes them tick, what keeps them going, what inspires and energizes them. Most of the people quoted were born in the 20th Century, and most are still creating.

What surprised me, as I read over the quotations, is the connection between words of young creative people and older creative people. It would seem that the human desire to express emotions and ideas through words and paint and music and pen and... yes, even bubbles... doesn't wane with age.

When I was a child, I tried piano lessons and grew fascinated with people who could memorize an etude or sonata; my skill was in *reading* notes, not *playing* music. I tried tap dancing lessons and quickly learned I could do the steps, but I didn't *feel* the movement. In school, I watched other kids draw pictures and wondered, why not me? And when I started to write as a grownup, the poetry just wasn't there. The secret that I didn't understand, until now, is that I could develop those parts of me; I could learn to *feel* music, *hear* oil paintings, *see* poetry in movement. I just needed to pay attention to what's inside me, what I *want* to do.

Some creative people have more than one talent; others focus on one skill. And yes, there are creative people using their gifts to cause havoc (I have not recorded their words).

As I explored the phenomenon from many directions, I picked up quotations that struck *my* creative senses, the words that have inspired *me* to keep going. You may find just the one that reminds you of your inner kid's lost aspirations. I didn't want to end the work — the adding and editing of this manuscript. Every time I read through it, I smile and feel uplifted and zany. Yes, zany! I get bumped up a notch!

You may recognize the declarations of some inventive, artistic people who express fears of "being found out", or of "being exposed as a fraud" — a fear that aspiring talent can identify with. Others tell how they overcame fears and developed a sense of balance between their *perceived* stardom and their personal lives. Surprisingly, a lot of them attribute their success to luck.

And no two are the same! As often as I listen to celebrated Originals, I am awed by the many ways their creativity is sparked, as well as by the many ways they react to the sparks. What binds them together is their love for what they do and a gnawing need to express themselves — their own way.

You may find inspiration here to encourage your own creativity, to continue to follow *your* instincts. You will notice quickly how many Originals speak of "learning to trust themselves" — to believe in what they do. Words that are often repeated reflect the notion that "I'm doing what I have to do, and loving it". Many of these are people who were talked into choosing a trade — "something to fall back on" or "what your grandfather did" — before learning they were much happier strumming a banjo or holding a paintbrush. Many of them changed their life paths when they recognized the songs they were meant to sing.

The comments recorded here share deeply emotional moments in all kinds of ways, funny and serious. Mystery still surrounds the source of creative gifts; perhaps it has something to do with the way they are shared. Quotations are listed in alphabetic order by last name, to soothe my jealous left-brain.

Sit back and absorb this phenomenon we call *humanity*. Creativity is what sets us apart from other animals; creativity is what injects zest into our lives, keeps us aspiring, keeps us sane, lets us sing our own song — loudly and clearly.

—Val Dumond, 2012

Val's Favorites

To give you a taste of what lies ahead, here are a few of my favorites:

> *They knock your socks off*
> *Then take our breath away;*
> *They go their own way,*
> *Find their own voice.*
> *They show us a new way of seeing*
> *And believing;*
> *They intrigue us,*
> *Entertain us,*
> *Inspire us,*
> *They are — American Masters*
> —**Public Broadcasting System** promotion

"Actors always have one foot in the cradle. We have to. Because we are in the business of transferring emotions to other people."
Sir Derek Jacoby, actor, at 61

> A little song
> A little dance
> A little seltzer
> Down your pants.
> **Chuckles the Clown,** from TV's The Mary Tyler Moore Show in 1977

"There is no agony like bearing an untold story inside of you."
Zora Neale Hurston (1891-1960) author

"Failure is being knocked down and staying down. Success is what you do when you get up."
Mark Ingram Sr., father of Mark Jr., first recipient of the Heisman Trophy for Alabama (2009)

"You can't create; you can only reflect creativity… we can't make raindrops or snowflakes, or the elements. We can only stay in tune with them."
Ahmad Jamal, musician, at 79

"Challenge is the only good reason to climb a mountain."
Sir Edmund Hillary (1919-2008) Adventurer, climbed Mt. Everest in 1953

"If you see something you want to do — and you turn it down, you think oh-oh!... Listen to the song of life."
Katharine Hepburn (1907-2003) Actor. Film, stage, TV

"If it's all beautiful, you can't believe it."
Ernest Hemingway (1899-1961) Author

"You have to be willing to commit bad words to paper. If I was telling this story, where would I begin?"
Melinda Haynes, Author, *Mother of Pearl, at* 45

"I thought about Trudi and had to write it down."
Ursula Hegi, Author, *Stones From The River*, at 54

"I live with the healing power of rhythm. The beating of a drum is musical, mystical, medicinal."
Mickey Hart, Drummer, The Grateful Dead, at 57

About his guitar: "This machine kills fascists."
Woody Guthrie (1912-1967) Folksinger, Composer "This Land Is Your Land"

"A mistake is only a half-step from the right note."
Miles Davis (1926-1991) Jazz Musician

"I need to write to find out what I'm thinking."
Larry Gelbart (1928-2009) TV Writer, Playwright, Screenwriter, and Author

"I learned not to ask questions, just to rely on intuition. Trust it. You need to be on your own to develop your own art."
Robert Franke, Photographer

"Most people go to their graves with their music still inside them."
Benjamin Disraeli (1804-1881) British Prime Minister

"Anybody that is good at anything does it for their own approval, not someone else's."
Michael Douglas, Actor

"If I had not written the books, someone would have done it instead."
>   **WILLIAM FAULKNER** (1897-1962) AUTHOR

At 102: "Life is so good!"
>   **GEORGE DAWSON** (1898-2001) WAS 98 WHEN HE LEARNED TO READ

"That's when you do your best work, when you're just doing it for yourself and your friends."
>   **DAVID BYRNE**, ARTIST

"Tying a knot is an adventure in unlimited space. What can be more wonderful than that?"
>   **CLIFFORD ASHLEY**, AUTHOR, ILLUSTRATOR OF *THE ASHLEY BOOK OF KNOTS* (1944, STILL IN PRINT)

(Creative people) "are not just curious about what they do, they're curious about all kinds of things. They're adventuresome; they are rebellious; they push the envelope. They tend to have a sense of humor."
>   **NANCY ANDREASEN**, NEUROSCIENTIST AND NEUROPSYCHIATRIST, AT 71

"Even crazy dreams come true — for air guitar players and other dreamers."
>   **ANONYMOUS**

BE CREATIVE! Add your own favorite music here:

Are You Singing Your Song?

> "Be a star in whatever you do!
> When you sing, you breathe in a different way.
> Life is breath.
> Life is music. So here I am."
> **Student in Singing Class**

~A~

"I never remember not being interested in sports.... I was doing something that I loved to do. That's what I would like to encourage people to do. Find something in this world and don't let anybody ever change your opinion that you can do it."
    JAMES ANTHONY (JIM) ABBOTT, ATHLETE, PITCHER, AT 45

"My colleagues at *The Times* have learned that I'm a multi-dimensional person and... they accept that."
    JILL ABRAMSON, FIRST FEMALE EXEC. ED. *NY TIMES, AT 57*

On the value of depression and the ability to listen: "We expect to be happy. When we're not, we become concerned. When you reach the crisis line (in writing and in life), you want to fix people in trouble. You can't. All you can do is listen."
    DIANE ACKERMAN, AUTHOR, *A SLENDER THREAD: REDISCOVERING HOPE AT THE HEART OF CRISIS*

"The family was into séances when I was a kid. I wanted to treat the material I was reading... and I also wanted to do a comedy, just like the old comedians, Bob Hope and Abbott and Costello, that flavor of comedy, but use real terms, real theories of paranormal research. Marry them up together, and there you have it: 'Ghost Busters'."
  Dan Ackroyd, actor, comedian, writer, at 60

"She (Junebug) made a choice every morning about the kind of person she was going to be. So many women do that. They wake up in the morning and say, 'Yes, things are hard, but I'm going to make the most of it.' That was her. And she's a hero to me."
  Amy Adams, actor, star of movie "Junebug"

"I've never become serious about anything. I'm still trying to figure it out."
  Bryan Adams, Canadian songwriter, rock star, photographer, at 51

William James Adams Jr. — See **Will I Am**

"I am someone who is dedicated to music purely through love and passion for it. It's an amazing feeling to wake up and want to go to school with kids who want to be something."
  Adele Adkins, British pop singer, *on applying for the British School For the Performing Arts.*

"I like working in a store. If Virginia Woolf had worked in a store, maybe she wouldn't have become depressed... I might rewrite my column like 20 times before I file it. You have to be very serious to be this kooky."
  Jonathan Adler, interior designer, furniture (with Simon Doonan, author, designer), at 42
  — See **Simon Doonan**

"Bubbles are very magical. Think about it. They float; they are colorful; they are these perfect spheres that are just mesmerizing."
  Geoffrey (Merlin) Akins, bubbleologist, "The Bubble Man", ("Gazillion Bubble Show" off Broadway), at 33
  — See **Fan Yang**

"Characters seem to ask, 'Take us by our shoulders and shake us up.' Use small talk to reach the point where the characters know what they've been holding in for years."
>   **EDWARD ALBEE**, PLAYWRIGHT, "THREE TALL WOMEN", "A DELICATE BALANCE", "SEASCAPE", "WHO'S AFRAID OF VIRGINIA WOOLF?"

"Survival depends on anger times imagination. Imagination is the only weapon on the reservation... the politics of dreams. Imagine a spring that mends broken bones. Imagine a drum that wraps itself around your heart. Imagine a story that puts wood in the fireplace."
>   **SHERMAN ALEXIE**, AUTHOR

"I need to reinvent myself (after 50). I want every day of my life to be fascinating, interesting, creative. I'm going to move forward from where I left off and I'm going to create a line of knitwear because this is something I've always wanted to do."
>   **KAREN ALLEN**, ACTOR, AT 56

"Yeah! This was the start of something BIG!"
>   **STEVE ALLEN** (1921-2000) HOST, "THE TONIGHT SHOW"; AUTHOR OF 50+ BOOKS; COMPOSER OF THOUSANDS OF SONGS; CREATOR OF TELEVISION'S "MEETING OF MINDS"

"These are beautiful spirits in black containers that any could admire. We're not blind to the beauty of other cultures, but what we need to do is become visually literate about ourselves, and we need to take the aesthetic in our hand and include ourselves. You can't get mad at another culture 'cause they're not singing your song. You have to sing your own song."
>   **TINA ALLEN**, SCULPTOR

"I can create beauty; I can give somebody a Wow! The way I think of myself is I make people happy. There is a general formula that I use in designing the nose."
>   **RICHARD ALLENBOGAN**, MUSICIAN, GARDENER, ARTIST, COSMETIC SURGEON

"When I put together a story, I grab everything I can. If I have to destroy my mother's life to write a story, I will... I love to write; I just love to write. If I didn't write, my soul would dry up and die."
>   **ISABEL ALLENDE**, AUTHOR, *DAUGHTER OF FORTUNE*

"In the novel..., I wanted the way I felt to mean something — and for everything in my life to change because of it.... Does it (writing) have to be good for something? Can't it just be good?"
        DOROTHY ALLISON, AUTHOR, *UNCLENCH MY FIST* AND *BASTARD OUT OF CAROLINA*

"It (singing) is like going to an analyst and just spilling your guts and getting something off your chest. Look! Here's the way it is!"
        GREGG ALLMAN, COUNTRY SINGER/MUSICIAN, AT 63

"Tijuana had some world class matadors (introduced with trumpets). I got chill bumps from that stuff and tried to translate the feeling of those afternoons into a song." (The Lonely Bull, 1962)
        HERB ALPERT, MUSICIAN, TRUMPETER WITH TIJUANA BRASS BAND, PAINTER, SCULPTOR, AT 75

"It's all surprise to me. If you know what's happened and what's going to happen, you can't keep your audience interested for very long."
        ROBERT ALTMAN, FILM DIRECTOR

"Word is a metaphor for the life of the imagination — the portable homeland. Take a detail of the past and make it much more grand. What is true and what isn't? Write about the stuff that isn't quite comfortable inside you, things that are hard to get at, and say, *Que yo scribo es loque siento, la verdad* (What I write is what I feel, the truth.).
        JULIA ALVIRER, AUTHOR, *TIME OF THE MIRAPOSAS*

"Design comes from the soul. It's like an instinctive reaction, the way you look at a painting and you love it or you don't love it."
        ANDA ANDRÉ, ARCHITECT

"If someone is feeling good on the inside, generally it will show on the outside and they'll draw positive experiences into their life. That's the way life works."
        STEVE ANDREAS, GESTALT THERAPIST, NEURO-LINGUISTIC PROGRAMMING PRACTITIONER

(Creative people) "are not just curious about what they do, they're curious about all kinds of things. They're adventuresome; they are rebellious; they push the envelope. They have a sense of humor."
        NANCY ANDREASEN, NEUROSCIENTIST AND NEUROPSYCHIATRIST, AT 71

"I had a kind of sweet four-octave voice that I could do so many calisthenics with (at 8)... It was quite devastating (surgery on vocal chords in 1997 at age 62) and I was fairly depressed for a while, and then it was either stay that way for the rest of my life or get on and do something." She has written 18 books, some co-authored with daughter Emma.
    JULIE ANDREWS, ACTOR, SINGER, AUTHOR, AT 72

"You give power to words by labeling them."
    MAYA ANGELOU, AUTHOR, *THE HEART OF A WOMAN*, AND *ON WRITER'S BLOCK*

"I'm moved by what I've done. You know, when you're doing it, you're so focused and busy, it doesn't really hit you until you reflect on it. I say, 'Wow, it's gone so quickly; how did I get it all in?'"
    PAUL ANKA, SINGER, SONGWRITER FOR 50 YEARS, AT 66

"You have to trust the people around you. People help each other, as it once was in America. People take pride in their honesty because it's the right thing to do. *Omoyar*, Japanese word for empathy, 'how another will feel if you lose something'."
    ANONYMOUS

"You don't just put those words on a page. You don't create a character, and that character does just what you want it to do. My characters wake me up in the morning, fussing sometimes. It's a very organic thing."
    TINA MCELROY ANSA, AUTHOR, *THE HAND THAT FANS*

"Editing means taking out things that sound great but don't add up to much.... Where did you get the idea? The family moved in with in-laws for a month while our house was being built; that became the premise for the book."
    A. MANETTE ANSAY, AUTHOR, *VINEGAR HILL*

"There's usually not any incredibly smart characters (in my films) because I don't know how smart people talk 'cause I don't talk that good.... Is it great to make people in the world laugh and give them moments of respite from the pain of this day, or is it just 'like me, like me'?"
    JUDD APATOW, FILM DIRECTOR, "FUNNY PEOPLE", AT 41

"I like to be in a place where there are different kinds of neuroses. In L.A. there's just one, and in New Mexico there's a lot of different kinds. So I get to move around them more fluidly... For the first thirty-five years of my life, acting was my reason for living, and if I wasn't acting or watching acting or talking about it, I felt like I didn't exist."
      ALAN ARKIN, ACTOR, MUSICIAN, AT 72

"One of the things that I so appreciate about my mom and dad, that they did so well was that they established what I call roots for us and, when the time was right, they gave us wings to make our own decisions."
      LIBBY GATES ARMINTROUT, DAUGHTER OF BILL GATES SR., SISTER OF BILL GATES III, ABOUT PARENTING

"It was my job to go in and recreate it (history), enter into that spirit, leave myself behind, and enter into the mind and society and outlook of the other. It is a form of what the Greeks call 'ecstasy'; it doesn't mean you go into a trance and have a vision; it means *ecstacis*, 'standing outside yourself, putting yourself behind'. And it is self, ego, that holds us back from what we call God."
      KAREN ARMSTRONG, HISTORIAN

"Actors don't retire. People who are in jobs they don't like retire. It's glorious! To work in a job you want and you like is in itself extraordinary. To be successful at it, that's gravy.... I was a little afraid of playing myself because I never felt very comfortable just being me. It's fabulous; when you get on stage, you can be anybody you want."
> *We're like birds who are perched on the limbs of a tree.*
> *When the time is right, we simply fly away.*
> *You must know the most important thing.*
> *Before the time when we must fly away,*
> *We have the chance to sing.*
> *Don't miss the chance — to sing!*

      BEA ARTHUR (1923-2009) ACTOR: STAGE, TV, FILM, AT 78

"It happens a lot of ways. Most of the time it's just spontaneous. Valerie will start to play. She'll take me over. My body. Her spirit just gets in me and I know what she's playing."
      NICHOLAS ASHFORD (1941-2011), SONGWRITER WITH WIFE VALERIE SIMPSON, MUSICIAN, AT 68

"Tying a knot is an adventure in unlimited space. What can be more wonderful than that?"
> **CLIFFORD ASHLEY**, AUTHOR, ILLUSTRATOR OF *THE ASHLEY BOOK OF KNOTS* (1944, STILL IN PRINT)

"It's the love that goes into them that's really the secret ingredient. When they get homemade cookies, they know that somebody cares."
> **SISTER MARY ASSUMPTA**, SISTERS OF THE HOLY SPIRIT, CLEVELAND, WHO HAS BEEN MAKING CHOCOLATE CHIP COOKIES FOR THE CLEVELAND INDIANS BASEBALL TEAM SINCE 1984, AT 56

"Saul Bellow had five wives, wrote 18 books, and harbored a thousand cranky opinions… but always there are magic acts of language, the long irony, the low laugh, the short fuse."
> **JAMES ATLAS**, BIOGRAPHER OF SAUL BELLOW

RICHARD AVEDON — SEE **JOHN LAHR**

~B~

"Can you remember futures before you were born? And pasts that haven't happened yet?"
> **JOHANN SEBASTIAN BACH** (1685-1750) MASTER MUSICIAN

"I was in need of income, with a record company near bankruptcy. Look, if it's a flop, you're going to go bankrupt anyway. But if it's a hit, you guys will have a business."
> **ROSS BAGDASARIAN SR.** (1920-1972) SONGWRITER, COMPOSER, CREATOR, "ALVIN AND THE CHIPMUNKS"

"It's the kind of thing that would have gotten laughed at in my family, and also where I'm from. 'You want to be an actor? Ya, me too; I want to fly to the moon. Now go and move that pile of bricks from here to over there.' That sort of mentality…. (At the beginning) I thought, 'This is fun. This is what movies are like.' Then I did three films that never saw the light of day and you come crashing down. That's what I like about it. It's always a bit of a crap shoot."
> **SIMON BAKER**, AUSTRALIAN ACTOR, MOVIES AND TV ("THE MENTALIST"), AT 42

"Diversity is the engine that drives this country. We are an immigrant nation. The first generation works their fingers to the bone making things; the next generation goes to college and innovates new ideas; the third generation snowboards and takes improv classes. We always need people who are pulling themselves up by the bootstraps."
    ALEX BALDWIN, ACTOR, AT 52

"You start with an emotion and go from there. Your emotion from one event can be transferred on paper to another event."
    MELISSA BANK, AUTHOR, *GIRL'S GUIDE TO HUNTING & FISHING*

"How do I define myself? Divinely impossible."
    TALLULAH BANKHEAD (1902-1968) ACTOR, CELEBRITY, AT 51

"I feel like a lion with the wind at my face. It got out that I was at Harvard. 'OMG, why is a model going to Harvard?' But that actually is a good thing. Because when people have low expectations, you're constantly going 'Ta-da!' They're like 'Wow!' It doesn't take a lot to wow them when they have low expectations. I think this is my life."
    TYRA BANKS, MODEL, BUSINESS OWNER, TV STAR, AT 37

"I don't think there is anything natural in being observed by other people. I have the need to express myself through my work…. That doesn't mean I have a need to enjoy the performance, or watch the performance or to enjoy the life of a performer."
    JAVIER BARDEM, SPANISH ACTOR, AT 41

"As soon as someone tells me I can't do something, I think uh-uh, obviously I can do that and I will do that…. There's a lot to do; I like this third act, so far."
    ELLEN BARKIN, ACTOR, STAGE AND FILM, AT 57

"You can always get better. Nobody can stop you from getting better. Nobody can stop you from trying to make something right."
    ROSEANN BARR, TELEVISION CELEBRITY, AT 58

"There's this crazy kid making art out of junk: spontaneous, childlike, bold, random energy…. Papa, you may not understand it (art), but one day I will be very famous."
    JEAN-MICHEL BASQUIAT (1960-1988) ARTIST, POET, FILM PRODUCER, MUSICIAN

"Fame is a weird head trip and you don't want to buy the attitude you actually need to be renting. What I'm focused on is making choices that lend themselves to a long career."
>
> **JASON BATEMAN**, ACTOR, FILMS AND TELEVISION, AT 42

At 100, on skiing: "It's a beautiful Sunday morning. I'm on the run and it's freshly groomed. Sanity goes out the window. You just point the tips and let them run."
>
> **LOU BATORI**, ATHLETE (SKIING, BICYCLING, AUTO AND MOTORCYCLE RACING), IN THE 70+ CLUB IN NUBS NOB, MICH.

From Bob Shieffer: "Amazing! She was paralyzed, wrote the book one letter at a time. Trapped inside a diving bell in the ocean's depths, he (the character) tells these tales without a teacup of sentimentality and without an ounce of self-pity. He found a way to share with us this adventure of the indomitable human spirit that lies deep within all of us, if only we choose to recognize it. If you aren't told *you can't* — you can."
>
> **JEAN DOMINIQUE BAUBY**, AUTHOR, *THE DIVING BELL AND THE BUTTERFLY*

BEEGEES — SEE **BARRY AND ROBIN GIBBS**

"Poverty was a constant companion, and it still nourishes my thinking; it still nourishes my compulsion."
>
> **HARRY BELAFONTE**, CARIBBEAN CALYPSO SINGER, ACTOR, SOCIAL ACTIVIST, AT 84

"Somehow we all knew what the goal was that we wanted. We knew we wanted it to be simple. We wanted it to be funky. And we knew we wanted to have fun. And we were willing to work hard."
>
> **AL BELL**, FORMER EXECUTIVE AT STAX, MEMPHIS RECORDING STUDIO OF THE '60S

"I've had people stand there and cry (in front of The Last Supper), simply amazed that you can do anything with lint. I'll never look at lint the same again. Art is in the eyes of the beholder. I love that.... If my dryer breaks down, my creation goes on hold, my Michelangelo moment."
>
> **LAURA BELL**, MICHIGAN LINT ARTIST IN BELIEVE IT OR NOT MUSEUM, AT 41

"When I am gone, let it be said that his sins were scarlet, but his books were read."
>   **HILAIRE BELLOC** (1870-1953) BRITISH WRITER OF LIGHT PROSE

"I was a weird kid… good at playing with numbers. I discovered that 2520 is the only number divisible by all the numbers from one to ten. I liked taking problems apart and not just doing the problem one way, but trying several different ways. Amazingly, I'd always get the same answer, and I found that consistency of math to be absolutely beautiful, and I still do."
>   **ARTHUR BENJAMIN**, MATHEMAGICIAN, MATH PROFFESSOR, HARVEY MUDD COLLEGE, AUTHOR, *THE SECRETS OF MENTAL MATH*, AT 48

TONY BENNETT — SEE **EVERETT R. KINSTLER**

"The girls were ripe for a change in literature. They were way overdue for a good, entertaining story that broke away from the old style of writing. I think Nancy was the character the girls were waiting for…. Nancy Drew means so much to so many girls and so many older women. It changed their lives and it gave them incentive to become active in professions and to go forward in life."
To a reporter, in confidence: "I'm so sick of Nancy Drew I could vomit."
>   **MILDRED BENSON** (1905-2002) MAJOR AUTHOR OF NANCY DREW MYSTERIES, PSEUDONYM: CAROLYN KEENE, AT 93

"I like bands. It's tough. It's the hardest kind of collaboration to have a band, but it's the most satisfying. It's a tough road. They don't make a lot of money; you travel a lot. I love jazz; I love swing; I love blues; I love fiddle music. I played in square dance bands when I was a kid too. It's jazz with a fiddle, Count Basie with a cowboy hat."
>   **RAY BENSON**, WESTERN MUSICIAN, "ASLEEP AT THE WHEEL"

"When you are creating, that material is sacred. It's between you and the page. Nobody else should be in the room. Just you, saying what you need to say."
>   **ELIZABETH BERG**, AUTHOR, *OPEN HOUSE*

"If we didn't hear some sniffles during the sneak previews of the picture ("The Way We Were"), we missed the boat. We saw the Kleenex come out and we knew it was OK…. The secret of a good collaboration is the secret of a good marriage. They're the same things:

there has to be respect; there has to be trust; you have to really like each other. Respect and trust!"
> **ALAN AND MARILYN BERGMAN**, SONGWRITERS SINCE 1950. SONGWRITERS HALL OF FAME 1980. Alan (at 84), Marilyn (at 80), BORN IN THE SAME BROOKLYN HOSPITAL, MARRIED SINCE 1958

"We are showing people it is possible to make music with things that you don't normally think of. You find small melodies wherever you look and listen. This is our message."
> **JÜRGEN BERLAKOVICH**, VIENNESE VEGETABLE MUSICIAN, AFTER 13 YEARS WITH AUSTRIA'S VEGETABLE ORCHESTRA

"I'm there to listen to them. So it sort of cuts through the B--S--. I open myself up and they go, 'Oh, you're interested in me!'"
> **BILL BERLONI**, ANIMAL TRAINER FOR STAGE, SCREEN, TV, ABOUT ANIMALS RESCUED FROM SHELTERS & TURNED INTO STARS

"All these books are written by people trying to figure out life; nobody has yet. Write your own book. Live your life for yourself. Figure it out for yourself…. Real writers are more interested in deep character than in high concept. As if by lightning, they illuminate. They shut our mouths and open a vein."
> **MICHAEL BÉRUBÁ**, PROFESSOR OF LITERATURE, PLAYS DRUMS AND ICE HOCKEY (NOT BOTH AT THE SAME TIME), AUTHOR, *LIFE AS WE KNOW IT*

"…kind of a surreal moment."
> **JUSTIN DREW BIEBER**, YOUTUBE SINGER, UPON BEING SIGNED TO A RECORDING CONTRACT, AT 15

"When I repair Grandmother's or Grandfather's pen, I'm actually giving back a piece of their heritage to their owners."
> **RICHARD BINDER**, THE PEN DOCTOR, REFURBISHES FOUNTAIN PENS, AT 65

(*About Magic Johnson*): "The one thing I know, if I ever had problems, if I call him (Johnson), he will be there. I got a lot of good friends, but one (is forever); it's him."
> **LARRY BIRD**, BOSTON CELTICS BASKETBALL STAR, MEMBER 1992 OLYMPIC DREAM TEAM
> — SEE **EARVIN (MAGIC) JOHNSON JR.**

20 / Are You Singing...

BLACK EYED PEAS — SEE **FERGIE** AND **WILL I AM**

"When I was a kid, I needed to sing because it makes me feel good about myself. It makes me feel good, period. When I was having a down day, I'd come down here (in Yonkers), right down to the pier and sing, like really loud."
    MARY JANE BLIGE, HIP-HOP SINGER, AT 40

BLUE JEANS (YES, THE KIND YOU WEAR EVERY DAY, OR WOULD LIKE TO WEAR)
Lynn Downey, Levi Strauss historian: "I can't think of any other clothing that elicits the kind of emotional response that blue jeans do."
Michael Allen Harris, California historian and author of *Jeans of the Old West*, searches old mines for antique jeans: "You can't research this stuff on the web. Nobody knows anything about it. It's like a mystery, you know, it's like being a denim detective."
Roy Slaper, Canadian sole designer/manufacturer and founder of ROY Jeans, men's custom raw denim jeans: "This is like a big deal for men because this is my denim."

"I can be six; I can be four; I can be a lot of different ages."
    JUDY BLUME, AUTHOR BOOKS FOR GIRLS AND YOUNG WOMEN

"It is a magical moment when you hear how songs have become a part of other people's lives in that way, and they do know all the words. It is incredible."
    JAMES BLUNT, BRITISH SINGER, KOSOVO PEACEKEEPER

"Write about what and who you know. Is this based on that person? Or... it's fiction informed by experience. The characters are composites of all kinds of folks I've known over thirty-plus years in the business."
    STEVEN BOCHKO, TELEVISION DIRECTOR, *AUTHOR, DEATH BY HOLLYWOOD*

"And that's how he got his face on the can."
    ANNA BOIARDI, COOKBOOK AUTHOR, GREAT-NIECE OF CHEF BOIARDI

"I make a damn good product and I want them to know who's making it."
    HECTOR BOIARDI (1897-1985) CHEF, CREATOR OF CHEF BOYARDEE

"If you can laugh at it, you can live with it."
>   **ERMA BOMBECK** (1927-1996), AUTHOR, HUMORIST, COLUMNIST

"When I'm out there, I feel like you can do anything. You can knock down the building; you're the best man there ever was for the job. There's that invincibility of being there. If the night's perfect, I'm not even there."
>   **JON BON JOVI**, ROCK MUSICIAN, AT 44

"I was popular within the group of unpopular kids (in high school). I was in the upper ten percent of the unpopular kids in school."
>   **ANDY BOROWITZ**, COMEDIAN, HUMOR WRITER, PERFORMER, AT 52

"I'd lost my identity. I'd say, 'Hi, I used to be Patty Boyd.' Until someone answered with, 'You still are!'"
>   **PATTY BOYD**, ON BEING ALONE AGAIN AFTER MARRIAGES TO GEORGE HARRISON AND ERIC CLAPTON

About her famous TV appearance. "It was actually experimentation. It's good to experiment. It's a bit like having a wee flower. If you put a wee bit of water on it, it actually blossoms."
>   **SUSAN BOYLE**, SINGER FROM SCOTLAND, AT 48

"At the very root, all art is entertainment that is fun. I'm just writing literature, and literature is an entertainment, at any level."
On art: Does it matter who made a work of art, whether they're a good or bad person, as long as the work of art itself is great? And I don't think it really matters."
>   **T. C. (TOM) BOYLE**, USC PROFESSOR, AUTHOR, BIOGRAPHER OF FRANK LLOYD WRIGHT, AT 60

"I am ridiculously in touch with my childhood. I have no problem remembering what it was like to be little.... I had that happy childhood, which was what makes me so shallow."
>   **SANDRA BOYNTON**, ARTIST, LYRICIST, GREETING CARD DESIGNER, AT 58

"Everyone must leave something behind when he dies, my grandfather said. A child or a book or a painting or a house or a wall built or a pair of shoes made. Or a garden planted. Something your hand touched

some way so your soul has somewhere to go when you die."
At 63: "I wrote *Fahrenheit 451* to teach people to love libraries as much as I do…. The ebook enables us to carry our libraries with us, and there's nothing wrong with that."
> **RAY BRADBURY** (1920-2012) AUTHOR, SCIENCE FICTION, FANTASY, MYSTERY

"I gave Emma a lot of my characteristics, which is drive, ambition, discipline, determination, and ambition, ambition, ambition. I'm still that worrying author who hopes the (next) book is going to work."
> **BARBARA TAYLOR BRADFORD**, AUTHOR, AT 76

"Remember: the joy is very important."
> **SWAMI BRAHMANANDA** (1863-1922) HINDU SPIRITUALIST

"At about 16, in school and doing some plays, it was almost as if a light went on, a couple of plays in. I internally thought: this is what I'm meant to do. I feel I've had the blessings of about 15 lifetimes as an actor."
> **KENNETH BRANAGH**, IRISH ACTOR, DIRECTOR, AT 51

(My first experience at) "acting was like falling in love and being utterly alone with God."
> **RUSSEL BRAND**, BRITISH ACTOR, COMEDIAN, AT 35

"What was lurking under that incredible self discipline was ambition. It was bravery. It was sending a message to her daughter: Don't give in. Stay in the game."
> **MARIE BRENNER**, AUTHOR *GREAT DAMES: WHAT I LEARNED FROM OLDER WOMEN*

Upon receiving an award: "You have high expectations when you go into something like… well, anything you go into. You think, oh, this could be good. Then every once in a while it transcends those high expectations and it's even better than you thought."
> **JEFF BRIDGES**, FILM AND TELEVISION ACTOR, AT 60

(At war crimes trial) "I hope to understand violence. In my life, I've been exposed to it: four wars, five executions, and I hope to understand the human being."
> **HOWARD BRODIE** (1916-2010) ARTIST, JOURNALIST, COURT ARTIST, AT 72

(I got into acting) "because you can create something from scratch, from nothing, and there's a fear in that and there's an excitement in that, so it's always changing. For me, it (acting) is like having fifty jobs. I like that, man. I get bored really easy. I do."
   JOSH BROLIN, ACTOR

"I never wanted to make it badly enough on someone else's terms. Show business wasn't that important to me — to be successful with what you wanted me to do. I sort of wanted to do it, and if it didn't work, I'd sell shoes. I'd do something else."
   ALBERT BROOKS, ACTOR, FILM MAKER, WRITER, AT 64

"There will come a time when passion is gone. There will come a time when ambition is gone. Curiosity will sustain you."
   HEYWOOD HALE "WOODY" BROUN (1918-2001) SPORTS WRITER TURNED ACTOR

"I can't read music. How I remember is visual, tactile memory in my fingers. If you think too hard, you can forget it. I guess it's somewhere in your subconscious. It's something like learning to ride a bike. You learn it so well you don't need to think about it anymore."
   ALISON BROWN, INVESTMENT BANKER AND BANJO PLAYER

"I think writing is incredibly transformative. It allows us to speak the unspoken, to take things that we've experienced and to make them real. And by writing our stories down, we make what happened to us and what we experienced real. And how that transforms you."
   SEAN McLAIN BROWN, GULF WAR VETERAN

"I've been through a bad experience and it has strengthened me and, with this new website (The Beast), I haven't been as anxious as I was when I went to do talk (shows), because at that point I hadn't had a failure…. Somehow it gives you a kind of inner strength."
   TINA BROWN, WRITER, EDITOR, PUBLISHER

"I don't see myself as an author of children's books. I make books for children, and in the most simple way. Children like that. When you make things as simple as possible, you make lots of room for their own imagination."
   DICK BRUNA, DUTCH ARTIST, AUTHOR OF CHILDREN'S BOOKS, AT 82

"How many people wish they had what I have, this surreal life where I go out on the road and I sing for ten thousand people every night. I come back on the bus and I have a beer with my mom and dad and the family. I have the best of both worlds. When I cover a great standard, conceptually, it's important for me to come up with something that's fresh.... I'm still in fear that it'll all go away. I look back now and I think of how naïve I was to keep going, and to think that this little break or this stepping stone was another stepping stone to where I was going. Because, if I look back now, if this was now, I mean, come on, Michael, this is never going to happen for you."
  MICHAEL BUBLÉ, CANADIAN SINGER, AT 32

BETTY BUCKLEY, JAZZ SINGER, ACTOR — SEE **JOHN SIMON**

"I guess I'm an equal opportunity abuser. My instincts are conservative in some ways, but I don't have any definable ideology. When I was in the White House, I had to... sometimes... pretend."
  CHRISTOPHER BUCKLEY, AUTHOR, SATIRIST, AT 55

"Why shouldn't I be normal? It's not about money. We had no idea what he (father, Warren Buffett) was doing, let alone he was making a lot of money."
  PETER BUFFETT, MUSICIAN, AUTHOR, AT 52

"I follow a dictum... if you're very rich, you should give your kids enough so they can do anything, but not enough so they can do nothing.... I'm betting on people."
  WARREN BUFFETT, FINANCIER, PHILANTHROPIST, AT 79

"If there's product out there with my name on it, it's me, so I want it to be good."
  TORY BURCH, FASHION DESIGNER, AT 45

"A teacher once wrote to me in school: 'Your penmanship is an assault upon the eyeballs. Your spelling makes me wish the Phoenicians had not invented the alphabet. But you write with such heart, I could not give you an F'. Writing is a mystical thing. I believe the gift is arbitrarily presented to individuals for reason that we never know. If a person is vain or arrogant with the gift, and presumptuous or imperious, it will be taken from him and it will be given to somebody else."
  JAMES LEE BURKE, AUTHOR, "DAVE ROBICHAUD" BOOKS

On history: "History is not just about 'was', but 'is'… conversely you begin to understand that if you know where you've been, you can sort of have a sense of where you are and where you might be going. I like to say your future lies behind you in the past you have yet to discover."
On Superman: "He's the offspring of all of us. I think the heart of the magic is the Clark/Superman/Lois relationship. I think my half of the human race (male) is always sitting there feeling like Clark Kent, wishing that you would see the Superman inside of us. And I think your half of the human face (female) has the enduring experience of having to put up with the Clark Kent in us (males) while you're searching for the Superman. It's a very fundamental human experience."
  KEVIN BURNS, DIRECTOR TELEVISION FILM/DOCUMENTARIES

"When you sing, you breathe — breathe in a different way. Life is breath, you know."
  LINDA EMILE BURNS, LED A CABARET SINGING CLASS

"I wrote because I had to write. I never wrote to make a pretty sentence. I wrote because I had to get it out."
  AUGUSTEN BURROUGHS, AUTHOR, MEMOIRS AND AUTOBIOGRAPHY

"What they (Hollywood) like about you, they fear about you. They think you're somewhat of a strange person, so they're always a little bit worried about what you want to do, even if it seems to be going okay."
  TIM BURTON, FILM-MAKER, SELF-DESCRIBED "CREATIVE MISFIT"

"We have not faced the existence of racism in this country. We're running out of words to express multiculturalism, diversity. We see beauty and ugliness in individuals and institutions; embrace and accept the ugliness and move beyond."
  JOHNNELLA BUTLER, PROFESSOR OF AMERICAN ETHNIC STUDIES, UNIVERSITY OF WASHINGTON

"That's when you do your best work, when you're just doing it for yourself and your friends."
  DAVID BYRNE, ARTIST

~C~

"Luck! I'm the luckiest person I know. My whole career, thinking where I came from, is a miracle. Do I believe in God? If you'd had my career, you'd believe in God. I certainly do. I'm not working to pay the telephone bill."
    MICHAEL CAINE, BRITISH ACTOR, AT 76

From Rhinestone Cowboy: "I've been walkin' the streets so long, singin' the same old song. That was just perfect."
    GLEN CAMPBELL, MUSICIAN, SINGER, GUITARIST, AT 75

"I make so many things in my life. When I was finished with one thing, very well, I start some other thing. I don't like to stop. I like to continually prove myself. I'm a gambler, you know…. It's extraordinary life. Yes. Voila!"
    PIERRE CARDIN, FRENCH DESIGNER, MAGAZINE PUBLISHER, TRANSLATOR, at 90

"Music has always been escapism for me. So I think writing inspirational songs is something that I need to do, and something that I feel other people will need to hear."
    MARIAH CAREY, SONGWRITER, VOCALIST, AT 38

"(The work of the novelist is) mixing *what we see* with *what we think* with *that which can never be*."
    PETER CAREY, AUSTRALIAN AUTHOR, WINNER OF THE BRITISH BOOKER PRIZE

"They laughed and sent me on my way. So I finally say, 'Well shoot! Somebody needs to do this, so I'm going to start trying to figure out a way to get this done. I think I could sell these.'"
    FRED CARL JR., INVENTOR OF THE VIKING RANGE, AN OVERSIZED COOK STOVE

"The show that I put on is always intended to be the most stimulating thing that can possibly transpire between one person and an organ. It's all a great celebration."
    CAMERON CARPENTER, PIPE ORGANIST, AT 29

"It is an interesting comparison between writing a book and building a house; they're very similar. Writing a book is really a tortuous process, and building a house was not as easy as I thought it would be.... What I am trying to do is to influence the way American power is exerted around the world. We must develop a way for American military power to be projected in a more enlightened fashion. We have to! Or more of the world than hates us now will hate us later."
  CALEB CARR, AUTHOR *THE ALIENIST, THE ANGEL OF DARKNESS, THE ITALIAN SECRETARY*

"There are no failures in Hollywood; only people who give up too soon. We actually are playing somebody who is a better guy than I am, and it raises me up by my bootstraps… when I walk away from the movie, maybe I am a better guy."
  DAVID CARRADINE (1936-2009) ACTOR "THE GOLDEN BOYS"
  — SEE **BRUCE DERN, RIP TORN**

"Never hold back. Use your power; put everything you've got in it… be a leader… avoid the clichés. If you want to be in there for a long time, you have to be an individual. Be somebody that nobody will ever forget. It's okay to make a mistake. It's what you do with that mistake. If you make one, you can make beautiful things out of a mistake."
  BETTY CARTER (1929-1998) JAZZ SINGER / MUSICIAN, AT 69

"When I was thirty-five, I was too old to get an agent. Forty is too old to go to Hollywood, but I'm proud to come to Hollywood at forty. Somehow, by hook or by crook, and God Almighty as my helper, I met Linda Bloodworth (Thomason, creator of 'Designing Women'). Success to me is wonderful, and yes, the fact that I was older allowed me to appreciate it, not take it for granted."
  DIXIE CARTER (1939-2010) ACTOR TV, "DESIGNING WOMEN"

On his 60-year marriage to Roslyn: "We learned a long time ago how different we are from one another. Also how, despite the inevitable incompatibilities during the day, we resolved many years ago never to ever end a day without being reconciled."
Interviewer: "So you always kiss each other goodnight?"
Carter (smiling): "Yes, at least."
  JIMMY CARTER, 39TH U.S. PRESIDENT (1976-1980), AUTHOR, NOBEL PEACE PRIZE RECIPIENT, WOODWORKER, PAINTER, WINE-MAKER, SUPPORTER OF HABITAT FOR HUMANITY, at 81

About the fascination of Wonder Woman: "I think it's that secret. It's that powerful, capable archetype of the secret self."
    LINDA CARTER, SINGER, ACTOR, AT 57

JOHNNY CASH (1932-2003) — SEE BILL FLANAGAN

"I'm a very structured person, so to bring my reason and discipline and my sense of poetry, to bring all those things to this kind of tidal wave of feelings, was very useful to me."
    ROSANNE CASH, SINGER, SONGWRITER, AT 50

"The more questions a work raises, the better the work is. It can be a joyful experience; it can be a serious experience. Success is waking up and going to swim, doing what you like, trying to live your life at your best.
    MAURIZIO CATTELAN, ITALIAN IRREVERENT, IMAGINATIVE ART JOKESTER, AT 51

"I can't do this sex bombshell anymore. They said I was scared of being sexy in my forties; I said I was not scared, I was terrified."
At 55: "I don't feel I'm working that hard; I'm having a great time. It's always that question: Can you have it all? Especially for us women. Well, I don't believe you can anymore."
    KIM CATTRALL, ACTOR: MOVIES, TV, STAGE, AT 40

"I consider myself a kid from Nebraska who was traumatized by meeting Bob Hope... when I was in junior high school... and deciding 'that's for me. I want to be in show business.'"
    DICK (RICHARD ALVA) CAVETT, TALK SHOW HOST IN THE '60S AND '70S, AUTHOR, HUMORIST, ACTOR, AT 74

"That's what you need in a credit crunch. You need everybody to realize that the pleasures of life, the real pleasures of life, are free."
    VERONICA CECIL, LONDON, CREATOR OF "PLAY ME, I'M YOURS", PIANOS-ON-THE-STREETS PROGRAM

"When color is at its richest, form is at its fullest. All the rest is poetry."
    PAUL CÉZANNE (1839-1906) FRENCH ARTIST, POSTIMPRESSIONIST (AT MT. ST. VICTOIRE)

"Do I outline? No. Absolutely not. Typically I don't do that until I'm well along in the book. I subscribe to what I call the Perdition Theory of Writing a Novel — which is that you just try to get as lost as you possibly can.... Jack Kirby (Capt. America) just never stopped dreaming up worlds. And that's what I think writing is all about — dreaming up worlds."

>**MICHAEL CHABON,** AUTHOR *THE AMAZING ADVENTURES OF KAVALIER AND CLAY*

"It's crazy and this is so much fun. It's my dream and it's what I've always wanted to do with my life."

>**GREYSON MICHAEL CHANCE,** YOUTUBE SINGER UPON BEING SIGNED TO A CONTRACT, AT 12

"It's the happiest I've ever been in my life."

>**CAROL CHANNING,** COMEDIAN, LEAD ACTOR, "HELLO DOLLY", AT 74

"Every black American is bi-lingual: street vernacular and interview talk."

>**RAY CHAPPELLE,** ACTOR

"Music is what I love; music is my life. I'm going to continue to do what I do because I love what I do. It stimulates me; it puts the voltage in me that makes me go. That's why when I go out on stage I give them all of me, not part of me, but everything I got, I give it to them."

>**RAY CHARLES** (1930-2009) JAZZ, GOSPEL, AND BLUES MUSICIAN

"I'm suddenly realizing... I'm doing the same thing today that I was doing in grade school... my passion to make everything as perfect as I can possibly make it."

>**TERRY CHASE,** OZARK MO ARTIST, SCIENTIST, COLLECTOR OF NATURAL HISTORY ARTIFACTS, AT 64

"Sometimes it does seem like every action you take, there's about eleven things that can go wrong. So you think, maybe if I don't do anything, nothing will go wrong. I doodled all the time in school. I think that was what kept me from going completely out of my head."

>**ROZ CHAST,** CARTOONIST

"This is a story of reconciliation from the Vietnam War, showing war for what it often is — a disagreement between friends."

>**BRIGADIER GENERAL DAN CHERRY,** USAF (RET.), AUTHOR, *MY ENEMY MY FRIEND*

"I know the audience. I know what they think, what they want; let's try writing a book. Opening lines raise questions; those questions are what propel the book through the narrative."
  Lee Child, mystery writer, at 56

"We survived on religion and humor."
  Chilean Miners, surviving 169 days underground in 2010, from unidentified miner

"More and more elected leaders know less and less of what they're doing. If I believed what I did ten years ago, something is dead. Propaganda is successful because people don't take time to unravel what's fed us…. Resist the unthinking society that blindly follows…. Focus on things that matter."
  Noam Chomsky, linguistics professor, M.I.T.

"I started to teach children about their roots, to keep an old culture alive. I don't look at his skin color; I look at, can he reach these notes? Is his timing good? And he has all that. (By traveling) we are promoting our culture. If we stay in Chinatown, we are only preserving it."
  Shirleen Chou, creator Purple Bamboo Orchestra, Oakland CA

"If everybody else your age is doing something very different than what you're doing, there's always going to be someone saying to you: *'You might not succeed with it. You might not make any money with that. There's always going to be some type of obstacle in the way.'* All those things will go away if you focus on what makes you happy."
  Kevin Clash, Sesame Street puppeteer (Elmo), at 52

> "A little song
> A little dance
> A little seltzer
> Down your pants."
>   **Chuckles the Clown**, from TV's The Mary Tyler Moore Show in 1977

"I love the way it was… 50 years ago… when everyone walked down the streets with suits and not jeans; it's just a kind of respect. I know nothing about, or very little about, today's pop art and different things."

From Ron Delsener, major music promoter: "He (Cincotti) is a writer also, which is good. So you don't just have a guy who's a copycat. And I think that's going to be his forte — to write in his style that's real classic. That's what he's going to be — a real classic."
From Phil Ramone, music producer: "You know, you can't fake what he (Cincotti) has. That's the key. He sits at the piano and things come out of him. I think that's rare."
  PETER CINCOTTI, JAZZ SINGER, A YOUNG MAN WITH AN OLD SOUL, AT 18

"Nikko Kazensakis (Zorba the Greek) said, 'When a man dies, a particular vision of life, which is his and his alone, dies with him. It therefore behooves every man to tell his story.' It's like the salmon coming back up the river to the place where it was spawned. You have to come back to where you came from."
  LIAM CLANCY, AUTHOR, FROM RING, IRELAND

"I'm a very fortunate man. I've had a second chance. I had to wait quite a long time, but that's all right; it's proof that it can happen any time…. At last I have a certain amount of continuity, a kind of tranquil kind of life where I am. I wake up and I know where I am; I know who I'm with; I know where I'm going, and I like the pace of it all. It feels very comfortable. It feels right."
  ERIC CLAPTON, MUSICIAN, RHYTHM/BLUES AND COUNTRY, WITH 16 GRAMMYS, AT 62

At 9: "I know what I want to be. I want to be a star."
At 50: "When I read it first, I said, 'I get this part' (a German lesbian heroin addict in the film "High Art"). As far as I am from it as a woman, it's closer to who I am as an actor, in that it is about transformation."
  PATRICIA CLARKSON, FILM ACTOR

"When I started out, I didn't care about money; I just wanted to get good pictures. I just thought of shooting pictures; I didn't think about anything else. There's a big similarity to me between photography and jazz. A musician has to master an instrument, an axe, as they call them, and photographers must master their axe with a camera. Be free enough to improvise. I feel that photography is jazz for the eye."
  WILLIAM CLAXTON, PHOTOGRAPHER AND AUTHOR, *PHOTOGRAPHIC MEMORY,* AT 76

"You remember everything anybody ever says."
>   **Pearl Cleage**, AUTHOR, *What Looks Like Crazy on an Ordinary Day*

"I am only human, although I regret it."
>   **Samuel L. Clemens** (1835-1910) HUMORIST, AUTHOR
>   — SEE **Mark Twain**

"You can either be the lead actor in your own life, or you can react to what others do to you. If I can feel good about what I'm doing, that's all I can do."
>   **Hillary Rodham Clinton,** U.S. SECRETARY OF STATE

"What's changed is perhaps a slightly brighter palette, a more celebratory nature to the work, because I was just so happy to be able to get back to work and to find a way to work again. Thankfully, if I'm only going to be able to do something that I used to do, I'm pretty lucky that it turned out to be painting."
>   **Chuck Close**, PORTRAIT ARTIST, RETURNED TO PAINTING AS PHYSICAL THERAPY AFTER CONFINEMENT TO A WHEELCHAIR, AT 79

"When I got to do Cruella, it was kind of a dream come true — to play a classic witch."
>   **Glenn Close**, ACTOR, FILM, STAGE, TELEVISION, AT 64

"Photography has a sense of mystery, of 'closed worlds and hidden societies', getting into peoples' lives to reveal something about peoples' lives and interpreting it. The rest of the world knows everything about America, but we know so little in general about the rest of the world."
>   **Jodi Cobb**, PHOTOGRAPHER FOR *National Geographic*, AUTHOR, *Through the Lens*

"I never thought I was there to change things. It's about asking questions and not knowing the answers."
>   **Leonard Cohen**, SINGER, "The New Songs" ALBUM

"The idea as a magician is to try to present your magic in such a way (that) the only answer is 'It must be magic!'"
>   **Steve Cohen**, MAGICIAN, AT 37

"I don't do quiet easily. (I offer messages on social issues) just because I love it and because I want to, and I can. The goal (in social awareness) is not to make you laugh; the goal is to provoke you."
    KENNETH COLE, FASHION DESIGNER, SOCIAL ACTIVIST

"I like to hold pencils and work with pen and charcoal and I have a real respect for the old masters of animation, and I want to hold onto that. I can see that in this age of technology it's slowly drifting away, and that saddens me. Because people are forgetting about the story and the character now; they're too seduced by technology."
    SHARON COLEMAN, ANIMATOR (DRAWS BY HAND)

"Sometimes people say, 'Don't you want to write the great literary masterpiece?' and I say, 'No, I love what I do.' I love writing about life in the fast lane. I'm not pretending to be a literary writer; I'm a story teller."
    JACKIE COLLINS, AUTHOR, NOVELS ABOUT LIFE IN HOLLYWOOD

"I wanted to teach the kids: You want something so bad? You put your heart into it…. God really works in wonders. He will provide you with the right people to meet and work with."
Student, after placing 11th in 2012 national competition: "Never give up. You can do anything in this world as long as you never… give… up."
    SHELLA CONDINO, SCIENCE TEACHER AT PRESIDIO (TX) HIGH SCHOOL, AEROSPACE TEACHER OF THE YEAR (2011), FOUNDER PRESIDIO ROCKET CLUB, AT 40

"I just like being around creative people, whether they be musicians, people involved with Broadway, or in movies. It's a big fantasyland… I'm so lucky that I get to spend so much time in that place."
    HARRY CONNICK JR., NEW ORLEANS MUSICIAN, ACTOR, GRAMMY WINNER, AT 42

"People treat you different if they know you're a writer…. You tell people you're a writer; they change…. You can't see people for what they really are. If you confront people when you're a nobody, people treat you in an altogether different way. And that's what I want from people…. I want them treating me like I'm a nobody (chokes up)… I'm never gonna give people any more of myself than what they read between the covers of those books…. Fools names and fools faces…

from childhood. Baseball: this is what I wanted to do, and I couldn't do it. Now I'm destroyed, a mess."
> **K. C. Constantine,** pen name for a mystery writer of *I'm a Nobody*. Won't be photographed or interviewed. Took him 16 years to get published — (circa 1975)

"The very place where safety lies for us is the thing that seems most dangerous, and that is having the courage to let people really, really, into what life has done to us."
> **Barbara Cook,** Broadway singing star, at 78

"If you can't get formal training, first find the logical way. And when you find it, avoid it and let your inner self break through and guide you. Don't try to be anybody but yourself.... (Duke) Ellington knew how to take what could be possible, to take something invisible, and make it visible."
> **Will Marion Cook,** jazz conductor/composer

"I'm learning new things every day on all the news shows I do, and when you're learning new things every day, it doesn't feel like work."
> **Anderson Cooper,** television newsman, at 45

"Beauty and the beast, a fairy story open to interpretation. There's one for each member of the audience. And it's the same with this. King Kong is part of our mythology; he is forever... a terrifying crowd pleaser from the start."
From **Kevin Brownlow**, *filmmaker:* "I mean, the whole thing is absolutely ridiculous when you think about it. The whole premise of King Kong is impossible. And the great achievement is every frame is so convincing."
> **Merian C. Cooper** (1893-1973) aviator, adventurer, film-maker, creator of "King Kong" (1933)

"At this age, I just want to do things I'm just personally obsessed to do. It's like being in love. I want to be in love with who I want to be in love with. Life is short and you don't want to be an old guy counting his last heartbeat, thinking about all the things you wanted to do that you didn't do because you were scared. What's to be scared of in life? In the end it all ends the same. Have a lot of fun!"
> **Francis Ford Coppola,** film director, business entrepreneur, at 68

Traditional closing message: "In parting, we wish you love, peace, and soul."
>   Don Cornelius (1936-2012), television host, "Soul Train"

"The truth is, I take what I do really seriously, really seriously. But what I realize is what I do ain't that serious. I probably play quintessential Americans, but it's kind of what I do. I am an American.... Music has to pass a test for me in order to want to share it, and I kinda in my own mind made up that the same way I do about the movies. I made up my mind that the music could hold them."
>   Kevin Costner, actor, director, musician, golfer, "born performer" (his words), at 52

"I set out to spruce up the whole dilapidated town. I can do something about this town. It's just amazing what a little bit of paint will do. It changes people's hearts. It's just what a community ought to do."
>   Jim Cotter, widower, volunteer house painter, Gloucester OH, at 81

"(Making money) is what I'm good at. All the successful people say this stuff that makes you just sound like such an arrogant joke, but it's my gift. Okay?"
>   Jim Cramer, TV financial guru, author

"I'm a normal woman… I have good days and bad days. I liked the way my skin looked, my body looked, but at the same time I love my life, and I think if you're happy in your life, it's easier to take."
>   Cindy Crawford, model, at 46

"To produce one nutcracker, start to finish, it takes two days.... I get so emotional when I see those dancers ("Nutcracker Suite") run across the stage with my nutcracker."
>   Glenn A. Crider, designer, artisan, handcrafter, owner: Nutcrackers USA

"I've been delighted that I've been able to be a journalist all my life. I think it worked out pretty well. And that's the way it is. There's reason to hope for the 21st century. And that's the way it will be."
>   Walter Cronkite (1916-2009) journalist, news anchor

"The best songs take you awhile to digest and no two people get exactly the same picture from them, because they insight a little fire; they ignite a little fire in your imagination.... (Music) just snuck up and kissed me on the ear."
>   **DAVID CROSBY,** MUSICIAN (CROSBY, STILLS AND NASH), SAILOR, AT 65

"It's the detours that help us remember who we are.... It's more about the experience of finally waking up and not feeling anything about it at all, not feeling anger or resentment or sadness or that phantom itch."
>   **SHERYL CROW,** SINGER, SONGWRITER, GRAMMY WINNER, AT 46

"Every time I am making a movie, I feel it is my first movie. Every time I have the same fear that I'm going to be fired. And I'm not joking. Every movie, the first week, I always feel that they could fire me."
>   **PENELOPE CRUZ,** ACTOR

"I think I developed my piano playing style through not being taught, and not being told how to play the piano.... It comes from not necessarily knowing what you're not allowed to do. As a child I was into music and I wanted to know everything. I think that's the point, to not look down on anything. If it's musical... if it makes sense in your head, then it's got to be good. Right?"
>   **JAMIE CULLUM,** JAZZ MUSICIAN

"What is this indescribable event in a dancer's life that arises, given all the shit, the terrible hours of work, the grumbling and malaise of a company, the point-of-vertigo fatigue when one day he drops it all and dances... and some internal, infernal hook holds one at a peak for those few seconds or, if you are extremely lucky, minutes...? Oh Lord, let me continue to live a little longer!"
>   **MERCE CUNNINGHAM** (1919-2009) DANCER, FROM HIS DIARIES, AT 53

"When you start to achieve, it's hard because people don't get their dreams... a lot. And to live a dream is... look at me... I have a life that is... I used to pretend all the time. I was a make-believer. To me that's acting."
>   **JAMIE LEE CURTIS,** AWARD-WINNING ACTOR, AUTHOR OF CHILDREN'S BOOKS, AT 51

"I had all that dark hair and blue eyes, a nice figure, jumping around, kissing girls, a lot of energy. Hip hop and jump around. How can you not go for me? I even went for me."
    TONY CURTIS (1925-2010) ACTOR, AT 77

~D~

"You got to move on. If you know where you're going, you're gone. Keep moving on."
    CYNTHIA DALE, SINGER

"This was a new adventure for me, to go into a realm of audio book reading, and having a whole host of children coming up to me in McDonald's and say to me, 'Can you order my hamburger as Dumbledore?'"
    JIM DALE, ACTOR, READER OF AUDIO BOOKS (VOICE OF HARRY POTTER CHARACTERS)
    — SEE **RON MCLARTY**

On Love:
    "Love is as strict as acting.
    If you want to love somebody,
    Stand there and do it.
    If you don't,
    Don't.
    There are no other choices."
    Tyne Daly, actor, stage, television, film.

About ballet: "There is that wholesome, healthy, athletic simplicity with a magical something."
    JACQUE D'AMBOISE, BALLET DANCER, ARRANGER, TEACHER, AT 76

DAME EDNA — SEE **BARRY HUMPHRIES**

"Making movies is the greatest job. I spent my teenage years, my formative years, hoping that one day I could be in a place I could make movies. It doesn't get any better than that."
    MATT DAMON, ACTOR, AT 40

"When I approach a song, I don't say 'it's a nice lyric', I try to relive a song. It's got to mean something to you, in your soul."
  VIC DAMONE, SINGER, ACTOR, AT 82

"By the time the performance comes, the work is all done. All the time I'm working on the next piece. Composers (artists) need to practice — by doing it. Composers practice their craft by doing it every day. Composing is a communicative art, aware of being on the receiving end. The act of writing is the greatest reward — the best thing I know of, next to praying. There is a basic human need to sing — the need to communicate, to write and sing and dance, and to remember. Remember we all belong to the same family."
  RICHARD DANIELPOUR, COMPOSER

"I can remember certain musicals and certain characters, you know, Fagan in 'Oliver' or Harold Hill in 'Trouble with a Capital-T' (Seventy-six Trombones), doing the whole song here and being able to pull them with me and then let them go. Pull them with me and let them go, as if they're on one end of this rope. I knew that at seventeen or eighteen."
  JEFF DANIELS, ACTOR, MUSICIAN, PLAYWRIGHT

"I'm not attracted to dark stories; I'm just attracted to the truth."
  LEE DANIELS, FILM-MAKER, AT 50

"The first time I heard a laugh on stage, it was like… BAM!... the light bulb!"
  TED DANSON, ACTOR, MARINE BIOLOGIST, AT 63

"A mistake is only a half-step from the right note."
  MILES DAVIS (1926-1991) JAZZ MUSICIAN

"What is there but a dream? Dream big and dream fierce."
  VIOLA DAVIS, FILM ACTOR, OSCAR WINNER, AT 46

"Life is so good!" (at 102 years of age)
  GEORGE DAWSON (1898-2001) LEARNED TO READ AT 98

"Calamity Jane is probably my favorite movie because that's the real me. When I was a little girl, I was a tomboy. I loved climbing trees, skating, and doing all the things the boys did. Yet, I loved dolls."
  DORIS DAY, ACTOR FILMS AND TV, ANIMAL ACTIVIST
  — SEE **MARY CLEERE HARAN**

"I just hate to shop with all that music in the background. And they're mostly drums. That pounding keeps the music from coming through. I like to hear the music."
    MARGRETA "BLOSSOM" DEARIE (1926-2009) SINGER, SONGWRITER, PIANIST, AT 58

"I don't think that's (gayness) the first adjective people think about when they think about me. I think dancing has overtaken the gayness."
    ELLEN DEGENERES, TV COMEDIAN, HOST, AT 53

"We are thin boundaries, lost into the dusty light, and believe everything we see on television news — all the pain, ecstasy, dog food, seraphic glitter, and baby bliss that falls from the air, and the terror that comes blowing through the fog."
    DON DELELO, NOVELIST, *MAO II*

"I just want to go on working. And when you get to 72, it gets trickier... because how many parts are there? The nature of an actor is to persuade an audience that they are that person and that the audience can believe in you as a person. Not see you; I don't want them to see me, Judi. I want them to see this person and believe in them."
    DAME JUDI DENCH, ACTOR, TV, MOVIES, STAGE, AT 72

"To get out there on the beach every day and lose every time, a drawing that's a mile across — it's a good fight. It's a worthy opponent.... (Sand art) can't be repeated. I like that aspect of it. When it washes away, that's just today's story. Tomorrow it'll be a different story."
    JIM DENEVAN, "THE SANDMAN", SAND ARTIST

"You know what the best part is? It's silence. That's the best part. When there are a thousand people and nobody is making a sound... because they're listening."
    BRIAN DENNEHY, ACTOR, FILMS, TV, STAGE, AT 60

"I continue to look forward to continually improve as an actor all the time, and that's enough for me. They'll ask, 'What's your favorite film?' The next one."
    BRUCE DERN, ACTOR "THE GOLDEN BOYS", AT 72
    — SEE DAVID CARRADINE, RIP TORN

COLIN DEXTER — SEE DCI MORSE

"No, I don't (get tired of performing). It's way too much fun. As long as I'm able to do it, you know, as long as people continue to come, I will do it."
      NEIL DIAMOND, SONGWRITER, SINGER, AT 67

"I went to bed every night with my jaw locked, saying 'Someone tricked me into believing that I had any talent.' And in the morning I would wake up with a terrible neck, saying to myself, 'We'll give it five more pages. You've already done nine years.'"
      JUNOZ DIAZ, AUTHOR, 2008 PULITZER IN DISTINGUISHED FICTION, AT 39

"There are 10,000 new words in this new edition, including: *nanoscale, ay, def, peloton, comb-over, brewski, headhunt, tweener, phat, botox, frankenfood, dead presidents, goth, dead cat drop, headbanger, McJob, mosh pit…*"
      DICTIONARY — 11TH WEBSTER'S COLLEGIATE (AUGUST 2003)

"I wanted to unpack my own baggage and do it in front of you… bad things happen to nice people: earthquakes, volcanos, fire, and more…. I had to write. Yeah, I can't think independently of writing. That's the only way I know how to think."
      JOAN DIDEON, AUTHOR, *THE YEAR OF MAGICAL THINKING*. ON COPING WITH THE DEATH OF HER HUSBAND

"For me, curiosity is the big magnet…. Good things come from making it up as you go along and being open to it and learning from it and scratching and bouncing off the walls and kind of putting one dumb foot in front of the other and reacting to the environment. That's fun!"
      BARRY DILLER, FORMER HEAD OF FOX STUDIO, FOUNDER OF IAC (INTER-ACTIVE CORPORATION), AT 62

"My work is a work… that reflects loss. (Romantic expressionist art) is not a movement. It's a way I would describe myself. I'm romantic about what I make — passionate and expressive."
      JIM DINE, ARTIST, PHOTOGRAPHER, SCULPTOR OF 3-STORY "PINOCCHIO", AT 73

"Most people go to their graves with their music still inside them."
      BENJAMIN DISRAELI (1804-1881) BRITISH PRIME MINISTER

At 75: "It's important to know the ending of a story. But the writing is a process of discovery. I'm discovering the same things the reader is discovering. (Writing) is not a job; it's a calling. Writing is so much a part of me, it's an internal government; if I didn't do it, things would fall apart."

At 78: "In fiction there are no borders. You can go anywhere. You can write as a reporter; you can do confession; you can sound like an anthropologist, a philosopher, a theologian, a pornographer — you can be anything and do anything.... Isn't that the idea? to write something that will last?"

  E. L. DOCTOROW, BEST-SELLING AUTHOR

About working in his studio: "It's really the only time when I can kinda have... like a clarity... and think about everything that's going on. There's a sort of calmness about being there and working, being in the studio alone."

  BRIAN DONNELLY, KAWS GRAFFITI ARTIST, PAINTER, DESIGNER, AT 34

"I love to take somewhat expected design motifs or concepts and tweak them. Good design should be chic and memorable. When I'm making a pot or designing something, I'm like pouring my soul into it; I lose sleep over it."

  SIMON DOONAN, AUTHOR, DESIGNER, AT 56
  — SEE JONATHAN ADLER

"Anybody who is good at anything does it for their own approval, not someone else's."

  MICHAEL DOUGLAS, ACTOR

"I look at the White House as a Shakespearian court, with power and movements, abuse of power, who is trying to grab power for the wrong reasons, and so I view it that way and I try and create a narrative for the reader. I don't want to scare people any more than I already am considered scary, so that's hard."

  MAUREEN DOWD, *NEW YORK TIMES* COLUMNIST, PULITZER PRIZE WINNER, AUTHOR, *ARE MEN NECESSARY?*

"(The recession) has kinda forced us to reset our thinking. But it's kinda fun. This is fun. You never figure it out. Every day there's a zig and a zag you gotta take."

  MICKEY DREXLER, RETAILER, CEO OF J. CREW

"In the incompleteness of the ruin is a blank for you to fill in, like 'what happened here? What does it mean?' It's a real engagement with the visitor."
 ARTHUR DRUCKER, PHOTOGRAPHER, "AMERICAN RUINS"

On swearing: "Language is a poor enough form of communication. We need every word we have."
On women suffrage: "Madam, you win the right to vote, but you lose the right to hide behind your powder puff or petticoats."
 HENRY DRUMMOND, FICTIONAL ATTORNEY IN *INHERIT THE WIND*, A PLAY BY JEROME LAWRENCE AND ROBERT EDWIN LEE, ABOUT THE SCOPES TRIAL

"Write in a cemetery. No one bothers you. A character has a good side and a bad side… use starter dough. Start with something and see what it becomes."
 ANDIE DUBUS, AUTHOR, *HOUSE OF SAND AND FOG*

> "When I use a word,
> It means just what
> I choose it to mean,
> Neither more nor less."
 HUMPTY DUMPTY, ABOUT DICTIONARIES, FROM *THROUGH THE LOOKING GLASS,* BY LEWIS CARROLL

"Always thinking. Always thinking, 'what's next? What makes what I do work?' It's this: what we're doing right now. Talking and listening. That's the beginning and the end. The beginning and the end of it is to be simple. I got things I want to do. I think sometimes the thing that comes around the corner and surprises you can be better than what you planned."
 ROBERT DUVAL, ACTOR

"Well, you never have enough (books) because there's always something in another book that you haven't read before."
 LLOYD DYCKMAN, CO-OWNER WITH WIFE LENORA OF THE "WORLD'S BIGGEST BOOKSTORE", IN PRAIRIE FARM, WISCONSIN

~E~

"As soon as we left the ground, I knew I myself had to fly.... 'I think I'd like to learn to fly,' I told the family casually that evening, knowing full well I'd die if I didn't."
        AMELIA EARHART (1898-1937?) AVIATION PIONEER, AT 20

"I talk about gifted people as if they're hustling politicos instead of artists, whose work teaches us to make imaginative leaps without which we'd be coarse, unreflective, unaffected, tragically unaware."
        DAVID EDELSTEIN, FILM CRITIC, AT 53

"If you want to learn anything — anything — you want to understand it; you've got to see it and record it and learn all about it.... Search for the unseen beauty in motion. You have to get up in the morning and want to do it. I used to tell people if you don't wake up at three o'clock in the morning and want to do something, you're wasting your time."
        HAROLD EDGERTON PHOTOGRAPHER, *STOPPING TIME, SEEING THE UNSEEN* — HIGH-SPEED LASER PHOTOGRAPHS

"Music is the common thing. It doesn't matter if you're a surgeon or on Wall Street or drive a bus, people here just talk about music. They start to act and think like a band."
        SPIKE EDNEY, CLASSIC ROCK MUSICIAN (WITH QUEENS), ON LEADING R&R CAMP, AT 58

JULIE EDWARDS — SEE **JULIE ANDREWS**

"Stepping into the world of theater, I knew I had found something special. I felt engaged. I was nervous. Every single day. I was stepping outside of my comfort zone... oh man, it was a rush! The actors I respect today are the ones who always took the hard road."
        ZACHARY DAVID ALEXANDER (ZAC) EFRON, ACTOR, SINGER, AT 25

"Joan was a peasant girl, remarkably courageous, remarkably sensitive. She was a great general and she was schizophrenic — so contradictory that she fell outside any category."
        PROFESSOR RICHARD EINHORN, COMPOSER, "VOICES OF LIGHT", ABOUT JOAN OF ARC

"No problem can be solved by the same consciousness that created it…. If you think something is impossible, don't disturb the person who is doing it…. Imagination is more important than knowledge…. There are only two ways to live your life: one as if nothing is a miracle; the other as though everything is a miracle."
        ALBERT EINSTEIN (1879-1955) PHYSICIST, NOBEL PRIZE WINNER

"When I started acting in earnest, at 12 years old, I really embraced it because, in a safe and contained environment, it allowed me to emote…. It doesn't always feel like there is a direct correlation between what you do and the effort you put in and the reception that follows."
        JESSE EISENBERG, FILM ACTOR, AT 27

"I am greedy. That's why I take so many chances. That's why I jump off cliffs. Because I just want to get out there and find out the thing I didn't expect and be surprised by that. That's the most thrilling thing. It has to come about through a certain amount of solitude, a certain amount of loneliness, a certain amount of human dedication to an inner life. It's when you get to the deeper parts of yourself that you're able to speak with a voice that transcends self and becomes a universal voice."
        KURT ELLING, DAREDEVIL JAZZ MUSICIAN, AT 42

"I took the energy it takes to pout, and wrote some blues."
        DUKE ELLINGTON (1899-1974) JAZZ MUSICIAN/COMPOSER

"It still attracts four million tourists a year. Not bad for a 75-year-old. Still standing tall!"
        EMPIRE STATE BUILDING BORN MAY 1, 1931, FROM CHARLES OSGOOD ON THE ANNIVERSARY OF THE 102-STORY BUILDING"

On writing: "I'm far far away, invisible. No one is listening. No one knows I'm there — gone. Forgotten."
    "If only there were a place
    Where the living and the dead could meet
    To tell their tales, to weep,
    I would reach for you,
    Not so you could forgive me, but so that you could know
    That I have no pride for what I've done,
    Only the wisdom and regret that came too late."
        EVE ENSLER, SCREENWRITER, "THE VAGINA MONOLOGUES" AND "LIFE SENTENCES" (ABOUT WOMEN IN PRISON)

"In a culture that is bombarding us every day — all of these things that are basically saying, you're not good enough. How about a message saying 'You're a wonderful mess. You are; I am; he is; you're a gorgeous human being. Embrace it.'"
      EMLIO ESTEVEZ, WRITER, FILM DIRECTOR, AT 49

"The more personal I get about a song, the more universal it is... I love people and what music does to them. It's that they hear it the way they want to. I give it to them and if they take that and that's their song, God bless 'em. That's great."
      MELISSA ETHERIDGE, SINGER, SONGWRITER, AUTHOR OF *MY LIFE AND LOVE AND MUSIC*

"Stare. It is the way to educate your eye. Stare. Cry. Listen. Eavesdrop. Die knowing something. You are not here long."
      WALKER EVANS (1903-1975) PHOTOGRAPHER OF THE GREAT DEPRESSION, DOCUMENTING AMERICA AS HE SAW IT

~F~

"My talent is more for making a bold iconic graphic that is provocative. The opportunity to share my work with people is what's rewarding, not so much the focus on me. I describe my art as graphic art with social and political messages."
      SHEPARD FAIREY, STREET ARTIST TURNED DESIGNER OF T-SHIRTS, SCARVES, TIES, BOOK COVERS, AT 39

"That's the result of an identity that has been flattened and suddenly is allowed to come up. I became myself, and it was not the person people thought I was. It was more intelligent, stronger, ravaged in its own way, but quite interesting. I think I've been very unconscious for a long time, and only now have I begun to get it. As long as I got it before I croaked, I think that's the main thing."
      MARIANNE FAITHFULL, R & R SINGER, AT 62

"I don't know what the hell I'm doing from moment to moment, and everything ends up being just a little bit better than the last thing. And each time I'm saying, 'How could it possibly get any better than this?' Then, you know, I turn the corner and there it is."
      EDIE FALCO, TV AND FILM ACTOR

"I like being the last thing you see before you go to bed. People watch our show and they fall asleep — to me. I want you to go to bed with a smile on your face and go to sleep and go, like… aaah."
  JIMMY FALLON, LATE NIGHT TELEVISION HOST, AT 36

"When I was eleven, I thought, 'I want to be a ventriloquist. I want to be the best ventriloquist that's ever lived.' (Now) I'm a comedian; I'm a singer, a puppeteer, a ventriloquist, an impressionist. It's like Wow!"
  TERRY FATOR, LAS VEGAS VENTRILOQUIST, AT 45

"If I had not written the books, someone would have done it instead."
  WILLIAM FAULKNER (1897-1962) AUTHOR

"It (singing and writing lyrics) came so naturally to me. It's weird that it never presented itself earlier."
From "Remembering To Breathe" (Dooji-wooji album):
 "Dancing toward your dreams can bring
 a breathless joy, but here's the thing:
 you've got to keep remembering
 to breathe."
  LORRAINE FEATHER, LYRICIST, SONGWRITER, SINGER, AT 61

JULES FEIFFER, SYNDICATED CARTOONIST — SEE **NORTON JUSTER**

"I don't really care about a lot of contemporary music, because there is so much that came before that is un-mined territory. And there is so much to discover. If there was a moratorium passed that no one was allowed to write a new song, we would have enough music."
  MICHAEL FEINSTEIN, MUSICIAN, COLLECTOR

"When I was five years old and running around telling everybody I wanted to write Broadway shows, it didn't occur to me it would take 56 years to accomplish that. But it was worth the wait. Look, Ma, a Tony!"
  JACK FELDMAN, LYRICIST, MUSICAL THEATER, UPON
  RECEIVING A TONY FOR HIS WORK ON "NEWSIES"

"I could always make music out of anything… I used to watch American Bandstand and what I would do is I would play along with some of the songs that they were playing and I thought to myself, 'If I can play these songs, I'm a professional.' My plan always was, 'I want to do this song better than the original.'"
  JOSÉ FELICIANO, SINGER, AT 61

"The stars align and sometimes there's a magic that happens with artists, and you just know it. You feel it in the room when you're working with somebody, that it's working."
      FERGIE (STACY FERGUSON), SINGER BLACK EYED PEAS, AT 34

"The book I wrote for myself. I didn't think it would ever get published. I wrote it for me. I think I have a certain restlessness. That's why I moved to the American West. It's a restless place, isn't it? Yah, I have that… like… awkwardness. Keep moving, rambling man."
      CRAIG FERGUSON, ACTOR, HUMORIST, WRITER, TV HOST. AUTHOR, *BETWEEN THE BRIDGE AND THE RIVER*, AT 45

On painting: "Art is poetry; poetry is art. In this country, you're pigeonholed. I'm both a painter and poet. It's just a different medium, but it's all the same urge, the same expression, the same message. Some days it may come out graphically; another day it'll come out in words."
      LAWRENCE FERLINGHETTI, ARTIST, POET
      — SEE **DONALD FRIEDMAN**

"I'm very proud to be a writer. I would not have any of the other jobs that I have if I had not been a writer first. It's great to be a writer, because you're at a wedding or something and you tell people you're a writer, they're less interested in talking to you than if you tell them you're an actor — which is great."
      TINA FEY, ACTOR, COMEDIAN, WRITER

"The first step is you're bothered (there aren't roles for older women). The second step is what do you do? I can learn to tell stories about people who are not me. I am not stuck inside my body railing against something I can't change. If I do that, I am making a step toward changing things. The stories I want to tell are all about women."
      SALLY FIELD, ACTOR, AT 60

"Bad guy roles: I think everyone has a world inside them, even people who do the worst things have all kinds of layers."
      ROY FIENNES, ACTOR

"I'd like to think I'm in this world for a reason — to make polo bigger and better. This is just the beginning… there's a lot more to achieve."
      IGNACIO (NACHO) FIGUERAS, ARGENTINIAN POLO PLAYER, RALPH LAUREN MODEL, AT 30

"You get a brand attached to you, whether invited or not.... I've learned that the baggage can be useful in the end, and you can't actually fight it, so you might as well make use of it."
        COLIN FIRTH, BRITISH ACTOR (MR. DARCY, IN "PRIDE AND PREJUDICE"), AT 49

"The key word for me is *Persistence*. Whatever you set out to do, you have to have a magnum passion to do it, and you've got to work beyond what you've ever dreamed you're going to do, to succeed at the level you want to succeed. Persistence, persistence, persistence!"
        VIC FIRTH, DRUMMER, DRUM STICKS MANUFACTURER, AT 77

"I like having the option of making up stuff and making it go a certain way. Life doesn't fall out like an entertainment. It really doesn't! And I like being able to make it go the way that I want since I hadn't been able to do that in my actual life. Please let me do it in the way I write."
        CARRIE FISHER, AUTHOR *POSTCARDS FROM THE EDGE*, AT 53

"If you're paying attention to what you care about and what you love and, for me, how the whole thing comes together, then it tends to work. The bottom line is really just numbers that repeat what's happening in the center. So you pay attention to what's happening in the center. And when that's right, the numbers follow."
        EILEEN FISHER, CLOTHES DESIGNER, AT 55

"(Writing) stresses the importance of looking at things differently. A cliché is anything you have ever heard before — and it's bad. You have to create your own language, fresh metaphors."
On the reality of characters: "Characters are like your friends. I spend more time with them than with my family."
        JANET FITCH, AUTHOR, *WHITE OLEANDER*

"Anyone who thinks Cash let go easily (after the death of his wife June) is wrong. Cash decided to use the gift God gave him and instead of sinking into grief, he began writing and recording with new energy. (He) took the loneliness and the overwhelming awareness of the love June gave him and put it all into his music. In many ways, Johnny Cash was just like us. But he could do something we can't do. He could take what we all feel but cannot articulate, and turn it, even the worst parts, and turn it into something beautiful that will live forever."
        BILL FLANAGAN (ABOUT SINGER JOHNNY CASH)

"As for sex, well sex is a perfectly respectable subject as far as Shakespeare was concerned, and I don't see why it shouldn't be so far as I am concerned."
>   IAN FLEMING (1908-1969) AUTHOR, JAMES BOND BOOKS

"Some of my first teachers were incredibly tough... that sort of process of dissecting and analyzing, being in a practice room and trying to figure out this incredibly mysterious instrument."
About crossing into other musical forms: "When we in classical music cross over, it's not over time been met with a large amount of success. They (daughters) saw me extending myself and taking a risk. And that's something you want your children to know about you, that you're willing to take a risk."
>   RENÉE FLEMING, OPERA LYRIC SOPRANO, CROSSING INTO POP AND ROCK MUSIC, AT 51

"Life is full of peaks and valleys. The more you contemplate how much you can grow, the better balance you will have to get through the valleys."
>   EUGENE FODOR, VIOLIN SOLOIST

"Easy on the students? No, I don't intend to be. I have to earn my keep. And just having pudgy little kids running loose, having fun, making noise, and me saying, 'Nice', and collecting money... what does it do? I'm here to teach them the only thing I know — ballet. If they don't want to learn it, what are we doing together? I can find better company than a 10-year-old.... I decided that I will help them grow up. And it seems to have worked. I teach them how to work hard, never give up, and many of them have learned how."
>   MADAME IRINE FOKINE (1922-2010), LEGENDARY BALLET DANCE TEACHER, CHOREOGRAPHER, AT 86
>   — SEE AMANDA HANKES

"Great drama is in the lives of ordinary people.... I often think, why did I choose certain things to write about, and I don't know that I chose them as much as they chose me.... You pick a little here and you pick a little there and you put it all together and make something new — like a collage almost.... It's like a musician; you train your ear. I'd rather listen than play baseball or climb trees or ride a bicycle. I just love to listen; I love to hear stories. I never get tired of them."
>   HORTON FOOTE (1916-2009) AUTHOR, AT 81

"You can have all the success in the world, but the confidence has to come first — inside."
>**JANE FONDA,** ACTOR, MOVIES & TV, ACTIVIST, AUTHOR, WORKOUT VIDEOS, AT 74

"It does feel like if Pink Martini was really famous, it would spoil it. Right now it's this somewhat undiscovered special treat that people who know about it are really supportive of and devoted to."
>**CHINA FORBES,** MEMBER PINK MARTINI, AT 41
>— SEE **THOMAS LAUDERDALE**

At 56, upon entering the White House: "They can kick me out, but they can't make me somebody I'm not. If we have to go to the White House, okay, I will go, but I'm going as myself and it's too late to change my pattern. If they don't like it, they'll just have to throw me out."
At 79: "I still get notes from women. They thank me from the standpoint of making it okay to go for treatment."
>**ELIZABETH ANN BLOOMER WARREN "BETTY" FORD** (1918-2011) FIRST LADY (1974-1977), FOUNDER OF REHABILITATION CLINIC THAT BEARS HER NAME

"I want them (the audience) to believe in the character. I want them to have the opportunity to feel what the character is feeling. I work desperately hard at getting the best I can out of every opportunity and out of myself."
>**HARRISON FORD,** FILM ACTOR, AT 67

"To be a novelist, you really gotta be lucky. You could work like the dickens, you could go to your study every day, you could have high aspirations, but you have to get lucky at some point. I'm really lucky to get to write books. Great literature, whether I could ever write it or not, meant so much to me when I was 19 years old. It changed my whole way of going into the world."
>**RICHARD FORD,** AUTHOR, AT 64

Quoting George Eliot: "It's never too late to be the person you could have been."
>**AMANDA FOREMAN,** HISTORIAN, AUTHOR OF *GEORGIANNA*
>— *DUCHESS OF DEVONSHIRE*

"My mantra is to be great every day. Because *good* is the enemy of *great.* To be good is so easy… you could be good with your eyes closed,

but to dig down and be great, that's gonna be harder. You gotta love what you're doing. It sounds so basic and so simple. But why do what you're taught to do? Do what you love to do."
    DAVID FOSTER, MUSIC PRODUCER OF STARS, AT 60

"He (David Bowie) was introducing me as a guitar player. (I thought) a pop star's career lasts eighteen months; a musician's career lasts a lifetime. And that's what I've learned."
    PETER FRAMPTON, BRITISH MUSICIAN, AT 61

"Will this war ever be over?"
    ANNE FRANK AUTHOR, *DIARY OF ANNE FRANK*

"I learned not to ask questions, just to rely on your intuition. Trust it. You need to be on your own to develop your own art."
    ROBERT FRANKE, PHOTOGRAPHER

"My dad, a pastor, had to push me to sing (at 14). I really didn't want to sing."
    ARETHA FRANKLIN, QUEEN OF SOUL, SINGER, JAZZ, BLUES, GOSPEL, AT 69

"If you would not be forgotten
As soon as you are dead and rotten,
Either write things worth reading,
Or do things worth the writing."
    BENJAMIN FRANKLIN (1706-1790) AUTHOR, U.S. *STATESMAN*

"If you don't write it, you'll wake up some day at 70 and regret that you didn't put some attention to this. Writing the book, I always felt like 'I'm going to write something I'll feel good about when I'm finished.'"
    CHARLES FRAZIER, AUTHOR, *COLD MOUNTAIN*)

"If I think I'm successful in what I've done, I want to look at it. It's not about you. It's kinda for me." (*About fitting stones*): "I personally can't live with a piece that doesn't fit to the other piece. If I do that shortcut, maybe you don't notice it, you know, consciously, but it diminishes that piece, and it's on a level that I can't even explain."
    LOU FRENCH, STONE MASON, ARTIST

"They (writers) found enormous pleasure in the act of painting and distinguished it very much from writing. Writers paint for as many different reasons as they write. They all have so much creativity. No one medium can contain it."
> **DONALD FRIEDMAN**, LAWYER TURNED WRITER, *THE WRITER'S BRUSH*, (PAINTINGS BY WRITERS)
> — SEE **KURT VONNEGUT, LAWRENCE FERLINGHETTI**

"I am a comprehensive, anticipatory design scientist. People say to me, 'I wonder what it would be like to be on a spaceship', and I say to you, 'You don't really realize what you're doing, because everybody is an astronaut. We all live aboard a beautiful little spaceship called Earth.'"
> **BUCKMINSTER (RICHARD) FULLER** (1898-1983) ARCHITECT, INVENTOR

"Everything in our features is... changing so you see it for a moment and then just have a memory. What we're focused on is making people stop and think, 'Wow I'm happy to be alive. This is a pretty neat thing, and it's free.'"
> **Mark Fuller**, ENGINEER, CREATOR OF FOUNTAINS (WATER ENTERTAINMENT TECHNOLOGIES)

~G~

"I'm not trying to write a hit song. I'm not trying to be famous. I'm not trying to sell records. I'm trying to write songs from here (heart). Now, after they're done, I have no problem putting my businessman's hat on and selling as many as I can.... Instead of thinking how great I've got it, I think about how much more work I have to do and how much more practicing I have to do to become a better saxophone player."
> **KENNY G (KENNETH BRUCE GORELICK)**, MUSICIAN, SAXOPHONIST, AT 51

"I was the kind of kid who wanted to be a writer.... I wanted to have written *Lord of the Rings*.... The joy of the monstrous is for me the joy of ghost fiction, the joy of vampires; it's the miraculous."
> **NEIL GAIMAN**, ENGLISH AUTHOR, WINNER NEWBERRY MEDAL, AT 49

"You don't start out to teach, but when you finish, you should learn something."
  Ernest J. Gaines, author, *A Lesson Before Dying*

"I'm not the greatest singer in the world; I'm not the greatest comedian in the world; I'm not the best impressionist either. But all those things put together with a lot of heart, a lot of drive, and a lot of wanting to be my very best, I'm here."
  Danny Gans (1957-2009) Las Vegas impressionist

"Was it scary? Not really. I knew I could fall on my face, but I've fallen on my face before.... I was forced to re-create myself. It happens in life. I am now an artist — a happy one too!"
  Gil Garcetti, L.A. lawyer/district attorney (turned photographer at age 59), at 64

"When I was on stage, maybe the first half a dozen times, experiencing this, was the only thirty minutes in my life that I didn't feel pain. And that was addictive."
  Melody Gardot, jazz singer, musician (seriously injured in an auto accident), at 25

Libby Gates — See **Libby Gates Armintrout**

"I wanted to be fashion designer; I became fashion designer. I think that everything is possible."
  Jean Paul Gautier, fashion designer exotique, at 59

"I need to write to find out what I'm thinking."
  Larry Gelbart (1928-2009) TV writer, playwright, screenwriter, and author

"My life is music, and in some vague, mysterious and subconscious way, I have always been driven by a taut inner spring which has propelled me to almost compulsively reach for perfection in music, often, in fact, mostly, at the expense of everything else in my life."
  Stan Getz (1932-1991) jazz musician

Robin: "We never questioned all the talk of music or harmony. We just sang what we felt."
Barry: "We were, in our own heads, already stars. It's the belief that you're already a star before you become one that makes you one."

Robin: "We don't know if we thought about reinventing ourselves."
Barry: "It was just about writing something that got us excited."
Robin: "…to be inspired."
Barry: We've still got a lot of music in us."
> **BARRY AND ROBIN GIBBS**, THE BEEGEES, SINGERS, SONGWRITERS

"Children can't achieve unless we raise their expectations and turn off the TV sets and eradicate the slander that says that a black youth with a book is *acting white*."
> **NANCY GILES**, TV COMMENTATOR

"Professional means to me not making mistakes. Anything that is really good, or extraordinary, or creative, comes from the possibility of failure. So when you eliminate the possibility for making mistakes, you eliminate the imagination… when you sit down and you have a piece of blank paper in front of you and then you create these personalities, and you can make them literally sit or stand or bend or talk, it's absolutely godlike."
> **MILTON GLASER**, DESIGNER, ARTIST

(What surprised me most about my success is…) "the fact that I was allowed to be me, but that only comes with hindsight. People ask dopey questions; they don't ask what they mean. What (they) really want to know is how come you're as black as you are? And you're here, and we're treating you like a white girl? That's what they wanted to ask me, but they couldn't quite get it together, because I was well paid and well taken care of."
> **WHOOPI GOLDBERG**, ACTOR, COMEDIAN, TV HOST

"Good seltzer should hurt the back of your throat; when the bubbles tickle the back of your throat, you know you've got good seltzer. If you grew up with this bottle on your table, you remember it fondly. It's not just a drink. It's a piece of history."
> **KENNY GOMBERG**, THIRD GENERATION OWNER GOMBERG SELTZER WORKS, BROOKLYN NY, AT 52

"I believe in young people living their dreams. I was just 10 when I decided I wanted to go to Africa, live among animals, and write books about them. I was 26 when my dream came true."
> **JANE GOODALL**, BRITISH ANTHROPOLOGIST STUDYING PRIMATES, AT 78

"*I love you more than God*, a daughter's search for her father. *I love you more than I love God*, and *I love you more than God loves you*. Such love is a form of aggression — a kind of imperialism. We will never be powerful enough to return it. And, our father is our God."
  MARY GORDON, AUTHOR, *SHADOW MAN*

KENNETH BRUCE GORELICK — SEE **KENNY G**

In the corner of one of his last drawings at age 82: "Aun aprendo" (*I am still learning*).
  FRANCISCO GOYA (1746-1828) SPANISH ARTIST

HANS GRAF — SEE "**THE PLANETS**"

"You can have the most beautiful voice in the world, and if you bring it to the stage and you have nothing to say, nobody wants to listen. Tell us a story. Say what you mean and mean what you say."
  SUSAN GRAHAM, MEZZO SOPRANO, OPERA SINGER

"Who am I? Why do I have these broken parts? People who interest me are people who have holes in them, people with problems. You get greater humanity that way. You grow!"
  BRIAN GRAZER, MOVIE PRODUCER

BENNY GREEN — SEE **BILLIE TAYLOR**

"Whether on a TV screen or computer or cell phone or toaster, the fundamental things still apply, or should: a love of story telling, a love of clear vivid language, a respect for history (the world did not start five years ago, even if YouTube did)."
  JEFF GREENFIELD, MEDIA CRITIC, AT 67

"(Art nouveau) is an attitude of mind as well. You can make a desk in any shape you want, as long as it has a flat surface, a drawer and somewhere to put your legs."
  HARRY GREENHOUSE, DESIGNER, EXHIBITING AT THE
  VICTORIA AND ALBERT MUSEUM IN LONDON

"I've learned a lot (from my dad, Joel Grey). I've learned how brutal this business is; I've learned how thrilling it is… to have opportunities made for you, and to relish and cherish that because it is like lightning in a bottle."
  JENNIFER GREY, FILM STAR, "DIRTY DANCING"

About Acting: "(As a child) I got laughs from the audience. I heard the audience cry. I had a death scene, and then there was an epilogue in which I came back to life. Now who wouldn't want to be an actor?"
About photography: "It was always something for me. I mean, it is just... somebody saw my work and they said 'you should do something with this.' And I said, 'I did. I took the pictures.'"
  JOEL GREY, ACTOR, SINGER, DANCER, PHOTOGRAPHER: *PICTURES I HAD TO TAKE* (2003) AND *LOOKING HARD AT UNEXAMINED THINGS* (2007), AT 75

"This world is attractive and mysterious and B.S., all at the same time.... I feel like I have to live every single day as if I'm going to lose it all tomorrow."
  KATHY GRIFFIN, TELEVISION COMEDY PERFORMER, AT 51

"I'm really hypercritical about it (my music). I tend to over-think things until the idea becomes pointless. So one of the other things that I've learned in my three-album career is to let things go. Sometimes you just need to let the child out into the world."
As a child: "I'd sit in the audience and I'd get chills and I'd say, 'Okay, if I can be the person who can make someone else feel that one day, then that's it. I'd be the happiest person in the world.'"
  JOSH GROBAN, SINGER, POP / CLASSICAL, AT 26

"Incredibly new possibilities start when the voice changes. As we have to say goodbye to our youth, we have to say goodbye to our young voices."
  AGNES GROSSMAN, ARTISTIC DIRECTOR, VIENNA BOYS CHOIR

JOHN GRUNSFELD — SEE **"THE PLANETS"**

"I mean, we weren't a band; we were just making shit up. That was how songs were created, that total free-form state where we just played and recorded and then excerpted and rearranged."
  TAYLOR GUARISCO, MUSICIAN WITH THE BAND, GIVERS, AT 24

"It's time my creative biological clock is telling me: the time is right to try something new. Ack!!!"
  CATHY GUISEWITE, ARTIST, ON DISCONTINUING HER COMIC STRIP "CATHY" AFTER 34 YEARS, AT 59

"For me, the critical question is: how do we as a profession avoid repeating in the future what we've done wrong in the past? Learning from mistakes means admitting to them first."
  SANJAY GUPTA, MD, NEUROSURGEON, AT 43

Printed on his guitar: "This machine kills fascists."
  WOODY GUTHRIE (1912-1967) FOLKSINGER, COMPOSER "THIS LAND IS YOUR LAND"

The Gypsy Robe: Singers and dancers that "give Broadway its body and soul", celebrate their role as "gypsies" in opening night rituals. It is awarded to an outstanding member of the cast, who dons it, circles the stage — and the show is blessed. At the time of the 2012 Tony Awards, there were 23 Robes, including two at the Smithsonian.
Chita Riviera (Dolores Conchita Figueroa del Rivero), "Queen of Gypsies", at 79: "I am a fanatic about this gypsy thing. I deeply believe you cannot have the kind of understanding you should have for the theater if you don't go through the ranks, that line."
Unidentified Recipient: Broadway to me seemed like a dream that was so far away that when I was setting goals, I thought, 'That's not a goal I want because it can never ever ever happen... and it happened, and this happens, so it's a little overwhelming to me."
  GYPSY ROBE, A TRADITIONAL CELEBRATION SINCE 1950, REPRESENTING THE DREAM OF BEING ON BROADWAY.

~H~

"I never appreciated how beautiful the world is until I went in the air. With aerial photography, you don't see any national borders; you don't see different cultures; you don't see different ways to worship God, things you get very preoccupied with when you're down on earth."
  ROBERT HAAS, AERIAL PHOTOGRAPHER, AUTHOR, AT 66

Upon release of "American Dreams" album, a collection of American music, following 9/11/01: "I felt they all belonged together for a reason, which is to tell a story about people who are free to dream and free to follow their dreams.... [The United States] should be viewed as a place that inspires people to be their very best."
  CHARLIE HADEN, JAZZ BASSIST, AT 63
  — SEE **KEITH JARRETT**

"When you're emotionally overcome is probably the only time you go deep enough to pull out the kind of things that are worthwhile."
  MERLE HAGGARD, COUNTRY SINGER, SONGWRITER, AT 73

LISA HAJEEB HALABY — SEE **QUEEN NOOR**

"If someone has a dream, and it isn't the norm of what others are doing around you, it doesn't matter. Reach for it; go for it; because I'm a shining example of that."
  DAVID HALLBERG, FIRST AMERICAN IN THE RUSSIAN BOLSHOI BALLET, AT 29

About *The Book of Ruth:* "I had trouble living with Ruth sometimes, because I didn't always like her."
About *A Map of the World:* "A friend of my two-year-old son died in the family swimming pool. The world is a disaster waiting to happen."
  JUNE HAMILTON, AUTHOR

"The things we're sentimental about are the fundamental things in life: the birth of a child, the death of a child — or of anybody — falling in love. I couldn't be anything but sentimental about these things. Write what you feel, and if you're honest, you'll have a winner. That feeling will come across.... People who deny themselves the privilege of dreaming are doomed to failure."
  OSCAR HAMMERSTEIN II (1895-1960) WRITER AND PRODUCER OF STAGE MUSICALS

"Sing what you know you're singing, and why you're singing it. People come to your world; you're not going out to convince anybody of anything. Go out there and be what it is you want to be in the aria at that moment, why that person exists. Relive those emotions and let people be part of your world."
  THOMAS HAMPSON, BARITONE, OPERA SINGER

"Jazz allows me to create something in the moment that comes really from me. For me, success was being able to create music that I felt good about."
  HERBIE HANCOCK, JAZZ MUSICIAN, RECEIVED 2008 GRAMMY ALBUM OF THE YEAR, AT 67

"What makes my books work? Dishonesty. Yes. I'm paid to lie on paper. It's true. These books tap into a common fantasy that many children and adults even have, which is 'what if there were no one to take care of me and I had to do everything myself?' Kids are used to be lied to by a hysterical overdressed adult."
      DANIEL HANDLER, AUTHOR, *A SERIES OF UNFORTUNATE EVENTS, BY LEMONY SNICKET,* AT 34

"You understand work ethic and you understand that if you want something, it takes hard work... it's not just handed to you. And that was something. She (Mme. Fokine) made you work for it. She was so pleased when you succeeded, but you had to do the work to get there."
      AMANDA HANKES, DANCER, NYC BALLET
    — SEE **IRINE FOKINE**

About Doris Day: "She had a lovely lullaby quality in her voice, and everybody responds to that lullaby thing, and that's universal."
    — **MARY CLEERE HARAN**, SINGER OF DAY'S SONGS

"I want my kids to laugh every day, and if they're not doing it themselves, I'll try to make 'em do it.... I want to have a good time myself. I don't want to dread going to work, no matter what the gig is. Selfishly, I will make sure I have a good time. How about that? And if they don't, well, tough beans!"
      TOM HANKS, FILM ACTOR, AT 54

Mata Hari took up dancing to support herself. After spying for the Germans in WWI, she was arrested in France and executed. When facing the firing squad, she blew a kiss to the soldiers.
      MATA HARI (1876-1917) DANCER, WORLD WAR I SPY

"People think I'm better than I am... I don't want to run out of ideas the next time I do a part and just phone it in, you know. So yeah, I'd rather the expectations stay low."
      WOODY HARRELSON, TELEVISION AND MOVIE ACTOR, AT 50

"It's like climbing the rock face of a mountain. It requires determination and stamina. You don't have a strong presence, you have to learn it, learn how to reach from the first row all the way to the last. You have to learn to say 'Here I am!'"
      JULIE HARRIS, ACTOR, PORTRAYING EMILY DICKINSON, "BELLE OF AMHERST", AT 80

"We (Peter O'Toole and Richard Burton) came out of the war. We grew up with death. We read daily — death. We all came to the same conclusion: we'd better enjoy it. I totally believe in the Shakespearean quote. I think it's from Coriolanus at the end of the play when he says, 'There is a life elsewhere and I love that life.' The *elsewhere* life which is doing nothing, going to a pub, sitting there, having a pint of Guinness, talking about rubbish… if I had my life to live all over again, I'd do the same thing. How can I have a regret? Wouldn't it be dreadful, sort of ungracious for me, to have a regret?"
    RICHARD HARRIS (1930-2002) BRITISH ACTOR

"I live with the healing power of rhythm. The beating of a drum is musical, mystical, medicinal."
    MICKEY HART, DRUMMER WITH GRATEFUL DEAD, AT 57

"After traveling around the world twice, telling strangers' stories, I've concluded the only difference between humans is that some people on earth live for purpose and the others… are men."
    STEVE HARTMAN, CBS JOURNALIST, "EVERYBODY IN THE WORLD HAS A STORY", AT 47

"I started studying (music) and after a while I got it. And after I got it, the larger it grew inside of me. It just filled me up. You stay with it long enough, you get it, because the soul is in the music. It's there."
    TIM HAUSER, SINGER WITH MANHATTAN TRANSFER, APPROACHING 60

"In the North there was Motown. They had a slick polished sound. And you go below the Mason-Dixon Line, down South, where the souls are raw. Raw sound! It was ours!"
    ISAAC HAYES, RECORDER AT STAX, MEMPHIS RECORDING STUDIO IN THE '60S

About building a terrarium: "I can take this home and I can take care of it. It's not going to go away."
    PAULA HAYES, TERRARIUM DESIGNER

"You have to be willing to commit bad words to paper. If I was telling this story, where would I begin?"
    MELINDA HAYNES, AUTHOR, *MOTHER OF PEARL*, AT 45

"I thought about Trudi and had to write it down."
URSULA HEGI, AUTHOR, *STONES FROM THE RIVER*, AT 54

"I'm a child of the Saturday-and-Sunday double-double features, so getting to work in the movies is a dream come true."
J. JOY HELLAI, MOVIE MAKEUP ARTIST

"If it's all beautiful, you can't believe it."
ERNEST HEMINGWAY (1899-1961) AUTHOR

"If you see something you want to do — and you turn it down, you think oh-oh!... Listen to the song of life."
KATHARINE HEPBURN (1907-2003) ACTOR, FILM, STAGE, TELEVISION, AT 94

"Performing is like floating above the audience, reaching into the heart of each person. You don't feel your body, only your spirit. You don't feel the floor. You just enjoy what you're doing."
PALOMA HERERA, BALLET DANCER, AMERICAN BALLET THEATER

"The secret of success of '60 Minutes'? Tell me a story. And that's all we do. Learn how to tell them a story and you'll be a success."
On his ideas: "I cannot explain where all those ideas came from. I have no idea. I know a lot and I have no idea how I know what I know. I just knew it and I don't know why."
DON HEWITT (1922-2009) CBS PIONEER NEWSMAN, DIRECTOR, PRODUCER "60 MINUTES", AT 86

"I thought simply I needed to go and read and maybe someday I would learn.... I wanted a story about how people are transformed by their circumstances, by each other, how they transform the world. She (leading character) mourned so we wouldn't have to."
ROBERT HICKS, MUSIC PUBLISHER, ART COLLECTOR, WRITER, *WIDOW OF THE SOUTH*

"With no formal training, I looked at clothes and figured I could do better."
TOMMY HILFIGER, CLOTHES DESIGNER, AT 57

"It (my career) happened rather quickly, before I had a chance to give it too much thought."
  MARG HILGENBERGER, TELEVISION ACTOR, AT 53

"A pamphlet you'll read once, but a song you can sing again and again. It stays in your heart."
His funeral instructions: "And let the merry breezes blow/My dust to where some flowers grow/Perhaps some fading flower then/Would come to life and bloom again."
  JOE HILL (1882-1916) WORDSMITH, ARTIST, MUSICIAN, UNION ACTIVIST

"Challenge is the only good reason to climb a mountain."
  SIR EDMUND HILLARY (1919-2008) ADVENTURER, CLIMBED MT. EVEREST IN 1953

"The things that have happened in my lifetime are… unbelievable. It's like the wheel was invented, you know. There's the automobile, the airplane, the radio, television, and the computer age. It's just really too much for one person to digest, you know. The time we're living in now, I don't understand. I try to go along with it, but more has happened in my lifetime, I think, than in the previous two billion years…. In recent years, with everyone telling me how old I am, I realize I'm getting old. I don't feel it. I don't live in the future or the past. I live in the present."
  AL HIRSCHFELD (1903-2003) ARTIST, CARICATURIST, AT 95

"The moment I earned a living as an artist, I felt I was rich, which I was actually because I was doing what you want to do. I mean there I was; I could look at the world, interpret it, and get paid for it as well. 'Well you're rich,' I thought, so what else would I want to do?"
  DAVID HOCKNEY, PORTRAIT ARTIST, PAINTER, AT 68

"I was shocked to learn that (he) was not the character I thought he was going to be. I had to work on a lighter book because I knew this book would take a difficult turn."
  ALICE HOFFMAN, AUTHOR, *HERE ON EARTH*, AT 48

"It has been twenty-five years since the play "Dream Girls", and I'm telling you, 'I'm not going'…. I sing it with a greater source of determination, a greater source of love, so yes, 'I'm not going', like never before, like never before."
  JENNIFER HOLLIDAY, ACTOR, "DREAM GIRLS", AT 47

"Folk music and spirituals helped move beyond my youthful anger and frustration, and become a more rounded, less afraid, more giving person, and that shows up in the music."
>> **ODETTA HOLMES** (1930-2008) FOLK SINGER, CIVIL RIGHTS BALLADEER, AT 78

"When you're always working in a new genre, it makes you feel young, because you're always a novice.... I'm very proud that I've been able to earn a living and apparently amuse or divert people for decades now, simply by arranging twelve notes and twenty-six letters in various orders."
>> **RUPERT HOLMES**, AUTHOR, MUSICIAN, PLAYWRIGHT, AT 58

GUSTAV HOLST — SEE "THE PLANETS"

"All of us are flawed human beings. None of us is perfect.... I just wanted to expand and evolve, not just be an actor. I just wanted to live more and broaden my horizon. So figuratively, this is what it is — a broad horizon. I've got a bigger life. It is not about a lot of money or success. It's nothing to do with that. It's just to have a more full life."
>> **SIR ANTHONY HOPKINS**, ACTOR, DIRECTOR, ARTIST, MUSICAL COMPOSER, PIANIST, AT 70

"Yes, it's still fun for me. I love it... Watching James Dean work was just a miracle. I'd never seen anybody improvise; in Shakespeare you don't go jumping off the page and saying other people's words."
>> **DENNIS HOPPER** (1934-2010) ACTOR, MOVIES/TELEVISION, ART COLLECTOR, AND PAINTER, AT 73

"All I wanted to do was to paint sunlight on the side of a house. If you could say it in words, you wouldn't need to paint it."
>> **EDWARD HOPPER** (1882-1967) ARTIST, ON HIS FASCINATION WITH SUNLIGHT, MOONLIGHT, NEON LIGHTS

"It's harder for me to sing 'Stormy Weather' the way I did it first than the way I sing it now. There's 40 years difference... in me."
>> **LENA HORNE** (1918-2010) SINGER, ACTOR, AT 64

"I've always been happiest when I am indulging the compulsion — and it (writing) is a compulsion to me."
>> **KHALED HOSSEINI**, AUTHOR *THE KITE RUNNER* AND *A THOUSAND SPLENDID SUNS*, AT 42

"There have been some mornings, at two in the morning, that I felt something, so I had to come here (to the piano) and work it out. Gospel is a cause, the end of the story for me. It's the reason I wake up in the morning and the reason I go the way I go."
        ISRAEL HOUGHTON, GOSPEL/JAZZ/ROCK SINGER, GRAMMY WINNER, AT 38

"The first expectation of a black artist often is something associated with rap, because that's what's most prolific out there right now. Mine is more of an orchestral jazz, the neo soul twist with a folk appetite. If I had to choose between acting and music, music! Easy choice. I control that; the music is strong enough to stand on its own. Now the question is, am I strong enough to carry it? We shall see."
        TERRENCE HOWARD, SINGER, OSCAR WINNING ACTOR, AT 39

"Edna says what they (audience) dare not say.... I had no intention of being an actor... I drifted into the theater. I still do. Every night, I drift in. I drift across the stage. I say to the audience, 'I'm making this up as I go along.' They laugh, but it's true."
        BARRY HUMPHRIES (DAME EDNA), AUSTRALIAN COMEDIAN, PAINTER, WRITER, RARE BOOKS COLLECTOR, AT 76

"There is no agony like bearing an untold story inside of you."
        ZORA NEALE HURSTON (1891-1960) AUTHOR

"Where I live is who I am, living on the Continental Divide... balance! I chose a small snug house with just enough space for me, compact, with doors I can close up tight and feel safe inside. And a wide yard to look out on with tall trees to shelter life. A patch of garden and surprises in the corners."
        PAM HUSTON, AUTHOR (LIVING IN COLO.), AT 30-SOMETHING

~I~

"Long ago, information was measured only in kilobytes. Then came megabytes and gigabytes, then terabytes, pedobytes, and exobytes. Today, with all this information flying back and forth on the Web, we will soon arrive at yodabytes. How big is that? Ten to the 24th power — 1000 billion trillion bytes!"
        IBM ad

"I am so far more secure and more grounded and more know who I am than when I was in my 20s. And that you can get, but only age can give you this."
>   IMAN, SOMALI-AMERICAN FASHION MODEL, BUSINESS ENTREPRENEUR, AT 56

"I have a special place in my heart for the underdog, the person who was told 'You'll never make it, that you'll never do it'. I cheer for the underdog because, guess what, we're all the underdog."
>   MO'NIQUE IMES, ACTOR, COMEDIAN, AT 42

"Failure is being knocked down and staying down. Success is what you do when you get up."
>   MARK INGRAM SR., FATHER OF MARK JR., FIRST RECIPIENT OF HEISMAN TROPHY FOR ALABAMA (2009)

"When you take a club back, or a bat, when you make that stride when the pitch comes in, there is no reality anymore. There's no sound. There's no wind. There's no time. There's no day. There's no night. (It is) a group of kids playing stickball."
>   WALTER IOOSS, SPORTS PHOTOGRAPHER *SPORTS ILLUSTRATED*, AT 65

"Use your uncommon sense and you surely will live an uncommonly sensible life. I always describe myself as the luckiest man alive. I'm doing what I know I'm meant to do. I love writing songs; I love singing them for people."
>   DAVID IPPOLITO, CENTRAL PARK SINGER, SONGWRITER, SINCE 1992

"I have a disaster imagination. In fact, much of what I'm criticized for by those people who don't like my work, is for having exactly that — an apocalyptic or Armageddon-like imagination. Guess what! I do… I feel that one of my strengths now as a writer is my readiness, willingness, my eagerness, to revise, to re-write the same sentence, the same paragraph, the same chapter until it is right. In life, it is better to put your head down, gut it up, and never give up. A guidance counselor once told me I had the lowest SAT scores in his memory. You live long enough, you savor those little cruelties."
>   JOHN WINSLOW IRVING, AUTHOR, AT 59

"How to write a novel: Ask: *how can you waste your life?* Answer: with self-deception and estrangement. Use emotions as themes. I'm obliged to follow what's inside myself. To map a plot, define the characters then shape the book (much like architecture). Consider: *there's a whole other life I should have had; I might have become a whole other person.* (What happened to change it?) *I should have become.... Did I let somebody down by not becoming?* Think about inside time and outside time; and don't waste time. It's running out.... Someday... I'll do something important. Today... I just go on living."
    KAZUO ISHIGURO, AUTHOR, *REMAINS OF THE DAY,* AT 42

YUSUF ISLAM — SEE CAT STEVENS

"I've fulfilled all my dreams as a writer. But I don't want the dream to stop. I love having this dream. This is the world's best dream. You don't ever want this dream to end."
    JANET/STEPHANIE IVANOVICH, AUTHOR, AT 56

~J~

"Actors always have one foot in the cradle. We have to. Because we are in the business of transferring emotions to other people."
    SIR DEREK JACOBY, ACTOR, AT 61

On Words: "I love words; words can be pulled to bits, put together again, elongated, invented — you can make words out of other words.
    Words have music;
    Words can be soft;
    Words can be sharp, like rocks;
    Words can flow like water.
    I love the music of words."
On Character: "That's someone you can like. That's someone who'll help you against a bully. That's someone who is happy. That's someone who smiles."
On Writing: "Paint pictures with words for those who can't see.... How can you write about things you don't know? The only thing that will stop me is word selection. I hate putting the same word twice on two lines. As for the rest, it's all there. Imagination. I dream about it!"
    BRIAN JACQUES, FROM LIVERPOOL, ENGLAND, AUTHOR
    REDWALL SERIES OF NOVELS, AT 61

"You can't create; you can only reflect creativity... we can't make raindrops or snowflakes, or the elements. We can only stay in tune with them."
    AHMAD JAMAL, MUSICIAN, AT 79

"I thought about it (writing the book) for forty years.... I thought about it for a long time. One of the points that I actually tried to make is that some things are worth doing for themselves. You can overdo it if you starve to death."
    CLIVE JAMES, AUTHOR *CULTURAL AMNESIA*, AT 68

"My rage kept me going. Something deep down in my soul said, 'Go on and cry, girl.'"
    ETTA JAMES (1939-2012), RHYTHM AND BLUES, JAZZ SINGER, AT 64

"Charlie and I are obsessed with beauty. An ecstatic moment in music is worth the lifetime of mastery that goes into it, because it can be shared."
    KEITH JARRETT, JAZZ PIANIST, COMPOSER, AT 66
    — SEE **CHARLIE HADEN**

"This language fulfills an emotional need to communicate how we feel and to affect other people. It's a part of being human. There's no other way to express surprise, joy, anger, frustration."
    TIMOTHY JAY, AUTHOR, *WHY WE CURSE: CURSING IN AMERICA*, AT 56

"Films are dreams in a way. They're made up of all your hopes and your joys and your fears and a combination of all those things. I think they are very personal. They are to me anyway... Just tell stories that move us to laughter and tears and perhaps reveal a little truth about ourselves."
    NORMAN JEWISON, CANADIAN FILM DIRECTOR, AUTHOR, *THIS TERRIBLE BUSINESS HAS BEEN GOOD TO ME*, AT 79

"I never thought I'd write a gospel type song like 'River of Dreams'. It just popped out and I'm singing, 'in the middle of the night... da tad da...' Naw, this is too simple. I'm not a gospel singer. I can't do this song. I'll just shake it off. I shower and I'm singing, 'in the middle of the night...'. I just couldn't shake it off. I guess I have to write this."
    BILLY JOEL, ROCK STAR, SONGWRITER, AT 57

"You gotta have hopes and dreams. That is defeatist thinking, I don't believe in it. You know what? That's for chumps!"
>	DOCTOR JOHN (MALCOLM JOHN "MAC" REBENNACK JR.), NEW ORLEANS LEGEND, SINGER, SONGWRITER, PIANIST, GUITARIST, JAZZ/BLUES, AT 65

"What intrigues me are cultures that are still very close to the land, and what intrigues me is what I can learn from those cultures.... The fact that you're camped out for months on end, you may be in a blind not for a day, but for weeks to get one photograph, but there always is that sense of the hunt, the hope that you'll get it, that there's light at the end of the tunnel. When you're in that mindset, the pain, all the problems you had getting the pictures, doesn't really matter."
>	CHRIS JOHNS, PHOTOGRAPHER, *NATIONAL GEOGRAPHIC*, AT 52

About Larry Bird: We'll always be there for each other. Forget the color of the skin. We're just alike. We don't have to talk every day, but he knows I got him, and he got me."
>	EARVIN (MAGIC) JOHNSON JR., L. A. LAKERS BASKETBALL STAR, MEMBER 1992 OLYMPICS DREAM TEAM
>	— SEE **LARRY BIRD**

"I've never wanted to be a celebrity. I wanted to be a racer. My deal is racing cars, and that's what makes me happy, what I am passionate about, and where my pride comes from."
>	JIMMY JOHNSON, NASCAR CHAMP 5 YEARS IN A ROW, AT 37

"If there's something I can do and I feel it should be done, I just want to do it. We want to be the pre-eminent African-American asset management company."
>	ROBERT L. JOHNSON, OWNER RLJ COMPANIES, FOUNDER BET TELEVISION CHANNEL, AT 59

"My worth isn't determined by the color of a medal. I was asked, 'How does it feel to lose?' If that's what people think, then we have it all wrong. I *won* a silver medal."
>	SHAWN JOHNSON, U.S. OLYMPIC GYMNAST, WON 2008 SILVER MEDAL, AT 20

At 40: "I wanted to be the best. I was not on commission. I made a salary. My inner motivation was myself, to be the best. The fire is there no matter what I sell. It doesn't have to be shoes."

At 65: "You want to sell something with a smile on your face, and they want to have confidence in you."
>   **LARRY JOLTIN**, NATIONAL SHOE SALESMAN OF THE YEAR (1983)

"We weren't just four guys who couldn't sing and play and couldn't act; we could do a little bit of each… and together we combined and made The Monkees."
>   **DAVY JONES** (1946-2012) BRITISH SINGER, ACTOR, AT 47

"I'm waiting for the role that I can say, 'Okay, that's my legacy!' I have a lot to look forward to — a lot!"
>   **JAMES EARL JONES**, ACTOR, AT 77

"Success is a strange animal, and if you don't have a serious grounded approach towards life, it can be just as defective as it is successful. (Count) Basie told me when I was 13, there's hills and valleys, and you have to learn the hills — that was a metaphor for success — but the valleys is when you find out what you're made of."
>   **QUINCY JONES JR.**, COMPOSER, ARRANGER, MUSICIAN, PRODUCER, AT 76

"I was always singing when I was a child. I always wanted to become a singer, but of course when you're a child, it's a dream. I dread to think about life without singing. It's a wonderful feeling to get on stage and pour all this stuff out and for people to go 'Yeah!'."
>   **TOM JONES**, POP SINGER TURNING TO GOSPEL AND PRAISE

"I don't know. I keep trying. And I try as hard as I can every time and, you know, they haven't figured out what I'm doin' to 'em yet. And I'm still getting away with it."
>   **TOMMY LEE JONES**, PRODUCER, DIRECTOR, ACTOR, AT 59

"To sing or play the blues, you have to have lived some, loved and lost, been betrayed, have felt the sting of things gone wrong — what you want is life slipping just out of your reach…. (If I never have another hit) I won't do anything. It's the same music no matter how many CDs you have sold. People come to see you. I'd be just as happy — honestly, just as happy — playing for five people for tips out on the street. It's what I do, what I'll always be doing, no matter what else happens."
>   **JANIS JOPLIN** (1943-1970) SINGER, SONGWRITER, ARRANGER

SARAH JOYCE — SEE **RUMER**

Feiffer (at 83): "This is why you do these things. You want to make a connection between yourself and some anonymous readers out there who you will be important to and who are important to you."
Norton (at 82): "People can read into it (*The Phantom Toll Booth*) what they like, and with my delight and my blessing."
    NORTON JUSTER, ARCHITECT, AUTHOR, CHILDREN'S BOOKS
    WITH **JULES FEIFFER**, CARTOONIST, PLAYWRIGHT

~K~

"The purpose of the story is to be the ax that breaks up the ice within us. What would be the purpose of happy stories? We read stories that remind us of our moment of fracture, that rub the wound; things don't go the way we want them to. Get on with it (the human struggle) in the shape you find yourself, and look what's been entrusted to you! Frailty, a few moments of self-reflection."
    FRANZ KAFKA (1883-1924) AUTHOR

"Color is the most exhilarating thing there is. As I get older, the blue gets bluer; the yellow gets yellower. Who knows how yellow it can become? For a rough draft, find out where things are, their relations, colors, and intensities. Use the known as a vehicle to bigger ideas. Forget about the tree. In the re-write, put in stronger color; make things memorable through color. Take your time."
    WOLFE KAHN, ARTIST, AT 69

Q: You want to save the world, don't you?
A: "That's an important thing to do, as long as I can remember. That's what the definition of life is. If you're not going to change the world, just go to sleep. Go hibernate."
Q: What is the process of invention?
A: "Looking at what everybody else looks at and seeing something else. If most people think what you're doing is completely normal, it probably is. Everybody else is doing that! Do something else!"
Q: Do you feel you're missing anything?
A: "Everybody is missing a huge amount because we all have so little time. In 50 years, nobody will know who the mother of that bride was, but Newton's Law will be 400 years old and Archimedes Principle will

be 2250 years old, and they will be as true then as they are now. They will be as important then as they are now."
>   **DEAN KAMEN**, INVENTOR, AT 50

"Those were very very rough times. I didn't know where the next paycheck was going to come from. I was borrowing money from my father (when) he said, 'Something good is going to happen. Don't stop believin', Jon.'"
>   **JONATHAN KANE**, MUSICIAN, MEMBER OF JOURNEY, WROTE "DON'T STOP BELIEVIN'", AT 61
>   — SEE **ARNEL PINEDA**

"(The kaleidoscope) represents the change we go through in life. There's never a moment that you're standing still. You're always growing; you're always changing. But the kaleidoscope represents that in the metaphor — for that life change and the chaos. It's controlled chaos."
>   **CHARLES KARADEMOS**, ARTIST, DIRECTOR, BREWSTER KALEIDOSCOPE SOCIETY

"To me it's individual. It's not about what you're wearing; it's who you are."
>   **DONNA KARAN**, FASHION DESIGNER, AT 61

"Kids in distressed families are great repositories of silence and carry in their bodies whole arctic wastelands of words not to be uttered, stories not to be told."
>   **MARY KARR**, ESSAYIST, MEMOIRIST, POET (*CHERRY, THE LIAR'S CLUB, SINNERS WELCOME*), AT 45

"One needs a great deal of quiet silent rage to write. Too much happiness gets in the way."
>   **SUSANNA KAYSEN**, AUTHOR, *GIRL INTERRUPTED,* AND *THE CAMERA MY MOTHER GAVE ME*, AT 52

"You set up a situation (a house stuck on the railroad tracks). Imagine the expected outcome. Then a train comes from the opposite direction… and misses. Sigh! Okay! Then the train comes down the original track and completes the expected outcome."
>   **BUSTER KEATON** (1895-1966) STAR COMEDIAN IN SILENT MOVIES

"I wanted to sing. I thought I was going to be a singer. I had tons of fantasies… and I still have aspirations…. I'm going to try as many things as I possibly can — except for flying."
    Diane Keaton, ACTOR, FILM AND STAGE, AT 64

"Life is either a daring adventure or nothing."
    Helen Keller (1880-1968) AUTHOR, POLITICAL ACTIVIST, LECTURER

"I felt comfortable doing the same thing over and over and over again, and that's one of the reasons I became good at cooking. I enjoyed the repetition; I didn't have to always be doing something new. I pinch myself every morning."
    Thomas Keller, RESTAURANT OWNER/CHEF, AT 56

"When I finished my first novel, I got a lot of hoopla. People would start to say things like, 'You're such a good writer, have you ever thought of writing a literary novel?' Then I figured it out. Oh, you want me to write the same book, without a plot. I just don't want to do it. It's not interesting to me. If you want to call me a genre novelist, great, I love it. I just write the same way I've been writing my whole life."
    Jonathan Kellerman, AUTHOR, CRIME FICTION, AT 58

"I think journalists should be as brave as Marines, and they should go out and tell us the story…. Those of us who were raised in the 'Lives of the Saints', perhaps we have a better appreciation of the full truth."
    Kitty Kelley, AUTHOR, BIOGRAPHER, AT 68

"As long as I have a voice in the U.S. Senate, it's going to be for that Democratic platform. The hope still lives, and the dream lives on."
    Theodore Kennedy (1932-2009) U.S. SENATOR, MASS.

"Dennis is written for me — something I enjoy doing."
    Hank Ketcham (1920-2001) CARTOONIST, JAZZ MUSICIAN, GOLFER, CREATOR OF "DENNIS THE MENACE"

"You dream it. My biggest dream when I was younger was what I wanted to have. I just wanted a sea of people to sing the words I was singing or that I wrote. It's really important to be who I am, and a lot of times people don't want you to be who you are. In some ways if you don't remain who you are, you're losing everything anyway."
    Alicia Keys, SINGER, SONGWRITER, AT 26

"Say it simply, say it truthfully, make it rhyme. I have a gift for music, and I've been lucky enough to share that with so many people. That means a lot to me."
>   **CAROLE KING**, SINGER, SONGWRITER, AT 64

"When I was a kid, I was a radio freak. I was a nut. It's easy (after 51 years); you love what you do."
>   **LARRY KING**, RADIO/TV TALK SHOW HOST, AT 76

"You don't need to see the whole staircase. Just take the first step."
"This is not a struggle for ourselves alone; this is a struggle to save the soul of America."
>   **MARTIN LUTHER KING JR.** (1929-1968) POLITICAL ACTIVIST, CIVIL RIGHTS LEADER

About writing of Africa: "A far away place I once knew well. I didn't have to be in Africa to write about it. I just had to be some place where I could think straight, remember, and properly invent. I needed the blessed emptiness of mind that comes from birdsong and dripping tree. People need wild places, whether or not they think they do, they do.
>   **BARBARA KINGSOLVER**, AUTHOR, *THE POISONWOOD BIBLE*, AT 43

"This healing happens when people are able to tell the truth, and when they are able to find words — human words — for human experiences. When we listen, we breathe in one another's words, and so a poem is about breathing, each others, and also communicating *with one another*. The only difference between vets of one war or another are where it took place or what war it was."
>   **MAXINE HONG KINGSTON**, POET, AUTHOR, LEADER OF WORKSHOPS WITH VETERANS, AT 67
>   — SEE **PAULINE LAURENT, SEAN MCLAIN BROWN, AND TED SEXAUER**

Kinstler, at 77: "I like it a lot — story telling. People look at a picture and it has to tell them something except what people look like. Whether you want to or not, you put it in some kind of text. When he (Bennett) sings, I sense he's richer and deeper. And that's taught me how you can eliminate what you want to say. How can you paint everything to say that particular thing? Absolutely, he (Bennett) is a master of that."

Bennett interjects, at 77: "It's musical storytelling."
Kinstler: "It takes two to paint a picture: one to paint and the other to tell him when it's time to stop."
> **Everett R. Kinstler**, Artist, Art Spirit Foundation, working on a film project with
> **Tony Bennett**, singer and artist

"I loved to sweat. I learned to try to make my tendus better, my pirouettes better, my jumps better."
> **Darci Kistler**, prima ballerina with NYC Ballet; teacher at School of American Ballet, at 46

"No king or prince has lived a better life."
> **Evel Knieval** (1938-2007) stuntman, daredevil

"I'm not comfortable with it (scrutiny). I think I can safely say I hate it. I think it's the idea of being watched, a sort of 24/7 surveillance. I think it's a very strange voyeurism; it makes me feel dirty. I don't want to be a part of that."
> **Keira Knightley**, actor, at 22

"Children's TV is a link between what we saw/heard with what we become. It is the link between what the world was and how it affected us."
> **Katharine Heintz Knowles**, U of Washington School of Communications, on TV and children

"Life without labor is guilt. Labor without art is brutality."
> **Kohler Plumbing** (Wisconsin Room) quotation of
> **John Ruskin**, English reformer

"I don't think writers who love what they do retire until they fall dead at the keyboard…. The imagination is a muscle, partly, and the more you use it, the easier it becomes."
> **Dean R. Koontz**, author, suspense thrillers and sci-fi, at 65

"Art requires that you bring nothing with it. Your own past history is perfect, so you only have future, and you only have possibility for transcendence. Today is the day, Jeff. Use today. Try to do something remarkable. Don't waste it."
> **Jeff Koonz**, artist, steel sculptor, at 54

"To be a planetarium director, you need college, but if you build your own, you can run it. It's going to just take off, like a rocket to the stars."
    FRANK KOVAC, ASPIRING ASTROPHYSICIST EXPLORING OUTER SPACE AT HIS KOVAC PLANETARIUM, AT 45

"If you're doing what you love to do, and doing it honestly and with your whole spirit and heart, then I think that's as good as it gets."
    KRIS KRISTOFFERSON, SONGWRITER, SINGER, ACTOR, AT 70

"I cared about language, the sounds and music of language
    I have walked through many lives,
    Some of them my own.
    And I am not who I was
    Though some principle of being abides...
    From which I struggle not to stray.
The spoken word is at the heart of poetry — It will always be so.
    I can scarcely wait 'til tomorrow
    When a new life begins for me,
    As it does each day...
    As it does each day!"
    STANLEY KUNITZ (1905-2006) POET LAUREATE, AT 95

"The painter paints in silence. Their work is silent. Their expression and interpretation are silent. Musicians create audible art; they express their art with sound, aloud. Listeners interpret in silence. Writers write with inner voices to produce audible words. Readers interpret with their inner ears to hear the inner voices."
    CHARLES KURALT (1934-1997) AWARD-WINNING JOURNALIST; HOST CBS SUNDAY MORNING (1979-1997)

~L~

"(Avedon) has the sense of the performing self. He understands that 'persona' means mask, and we walk around with masks, and his gift is being able to penetrate that mask — to see the essential thing that it hides."
    JOHN LAHR, SON OF **BERT LAHR** (1895-1967) *ON A PHOTO TAKEN BY RICHARD AVEDON THAT CAPTURED HIS FATHER'S ESSENCE*

"But a woman, ah a woman, from good schools and a good family, who achieved it all so easily. No, that woman has to publicly suffer so that we know she's real."
>   **CHRISTINE LAHTI**, ACTOR, FILM DIRECTOR, COMMENTING ON WENDY WASSERSTEIN'S "AN AMERICAN DAUGHTER", AT 59

"I am not afraid of failure. No. I'm already a winner. I'm 51 years old and look what I have behind me. Taking a risk has always been a part of first my DNA and then Cirque DNA. I believe you don't achieve great things if you don't take great risks."
About his trip into space in a Russian rocket in 2009: "I like to live my fairytale. Fairytales are possible."
>   **GUY LALIBERTÉ**, CANADIAN CEO CIRQUE DU SOLEIL, ENTREPRENEUR, PHILANTHROPIST, POKER PLAYER, AT 51

"In the act of complaining, you write around the problem… I tried to write around a character. I didn't know if he'd be good or bad for her."
>   **WALLY LAMB**, AUTHOR, *I KNOW THIS MUCH IS TRUE* AND *SHE CAME UNDONE*

"Coming from our kitchen in New Orleans, then to be able to play a festival like this, being able to reach people, I couldn't have dreamed of a better life."
>   **TIFFANY LAMSON**, SINGER, MUSICIAN WITH THE BAND, GIVERS, AT 23

"I decided finally, there is a Heifitz; I will never be one. I put the violin down and… got into the kitchen."
>   **GEORGE LANG** (1924-2011), HUNGARIAN BORN VIOLINIST, RESTAURATEUR (CAFÉ DES ARTISTES, NY CITY), AT 61

"It's kinda like I was born to be a singer, like a lemon tree was born to make lemons. And I'm lucky that's what I'm able to do."
>   **K. D. LANG**, MUSICIAN, SINGER, AT 46

"The good music is like turning you to a journey because sometimes the music can stop your breath. If you don't want to be famous, you can sleep. If you want to be famous, you must get up. If you have a son, you want him to be a dragon; if you have a daughter, you want her to be a phoenix — the best!"
>   **LANG LANG**, PIANIST, AT 20

"What I try to do with the origami figure is to create the same emotional response when you see the origami that I experience when I see the actual subject."
    ROBERT LANG, ENGINEER, PHYSICIST, AUTHOR,
    THE COMPLETE BOOK OF ORIGAMI

"I think you have to give up this concern about what people are going to think of you. I think that was instilled in me as a child — that thing about being brave, trying to be brave at least."
    JESSICA LANGE, ACTOR, PHOTOGRAPHER, AT 58

About personal life: "It's just none of your business. And it's none of the public's business. What I owe the public is a great performance, and I hope that I give my absolute *all* to the public."
    FRANK LANGELLA, ACTOR, MOVIES AND STAGE, AT 71

"There are times when you walk into that dressing room and think 'I can't do this; I cannot do this.' It's a curious thing, when you sit down in front of that mirror and you pick up that first piece of makeup and you start to apply it, suddenly you transform yourself into that person who *is* capable of going onstage and delivering that performance. This is the only thing that I know how to do, and I think that is the reason I've stayed with it all my life. I only come alive when I'm working."
    ANGELA LANSBURY, ACTOR ON STAGE, TV, FILMS SINCE 1944
    (SIX TONY AWARDS), AT 84

"That race was proof that anything can happen. As unscientific as it may sound, I do believe in magic, magic that defies all logic. I've seen it in medicine and I saw it here at the Belmont in 1973."
    DR. JOHN LaPOOK, RACEHORSE OWNER (SECRETARIAT, BIG
    RED, WINNER OF TRIPLE CROWN 1973), AT 54

"I'm all about what really reflects real life, and I feel like this is who I am. If I feel like training and dropping some pounds for my health, I'll do that. If I eat a little extra mac and cheese, then, hey, it was good."
    QUEEN LATIFAH, ENTERTAINER, SINGER, FILMS, TV, AT 37
    — SEE **DANA OWENS**

"It's old-fashioned symphonic global pop."
    THOMAS LAUDERDALE, LINGUISTIC MUSICIAN, FOUNDER PINK
    MARTINI, AT 41
    — SEE **CHINA FORBES**

"I started writing to heal myself and to tell a story I had never told before. Writing became a container that could hold all my pain. It was like writing with a vessel, and I could just keep putting more pain in that vessel, and writing could hold it all. Writing didn't tell me to 'get over it and get better and get married again'. Writing just said, 'Tell me more. More. Give me more of your pain. I'm here to receive it.' And it was such a gift to find writing."
> PAULINE LAURENT, VIETNAM WAR WIDOW, WHO REACTED WITH SILENCE FOR 25 YEARS TO HUSBAND'S DEATH JUST BEFORE BIRTH OF A CHILD (*VETERANS OF WAR, VETERANS OF PEACE*)

"At first it (being called *mean*) bothered me, and now it doesn't, because I know who and what I am. I have a saying: if you believe it, you're dead. And I think people who believe in their success, or in their reviews, or in anything but what they are doing, are unfortunate."
> ARTHUR LAURENTS, BROADWAY PLAYWRIGHT, PRODUCER, DIRECTOR, AT 91

"Probably House (TV character) has given me a confidence as a performer that I didn't have before. It took me a long time to find."
> HUGH LAURIE, BRITISH ACTOR, JAZZ MUSICIAN, AT 52

"I feel frustrated a lot of times because I just say, 'What the hell is the use of writing about it or talking about it. You have to go look at it!' And if you can't see it when you're looking at it, you never will."
> JOHN LAUTNER, ARCHITECT OF DISTINCTIVE HOLLYWOOD HOMES; PROTÉGÉ OF FRANK LLOYD WRIGHT

"I want to be lonely again. Lonely's not bad."
> CHRISTINE LAVIN, MUSICAL STORYTELLER, "BITCHIN' BABES"

JEROME LAWRENCE, PLAYWRIGHT — SEE **HENRY DRUMMOND**

"If a writer asked me for the best advice, I'd say, 'Write!' Taking a hint from that, I'd say, 'Do!' I wouldn't trade anything. If things are right at any given moment, everything that led up to it has to have been right…. I'm occupied with now and next. There's no slowing down. What I want to do is wake up every morning of my life to do something that I think matters."
> NORMAN LEAR, PRODUCER OF TV, MOVIES, MUSIC, AT 86

"How do I eat it (pastrami sandwich)? Anyone who takes a lean pastrami sandwich, they think it's healthier, not better, doesn't taste as good. (It takes) fatty to do it, do it right."
    JACK LEBEWOHL, OWNER, SECOND AVENUE DELI, NYC, AT 62

"Women's history began in the mid-1960s. We ransacked the past for role models, rushing to find heroines. In social history, we found the 'normal woman doing traditional women's work', in other words, the invisible woman. In politics, women were volunteers working behind the scenes. We had to weave together the 'history of women' with 'real history'. Until then, women were kept in a box, a sidebar in textbooks and newspapers. After all, history is about great leaders — men — or is it? What matters in history? What is history? Surely not a pure flow of men's lives."
    SUZANNE LEBSOCK, PROFESSOR OF WOMEN'S HISTORY, UNIVERSITY OF WASHINGTON

"If you tell a good intricate story without a lot of meat and potatoes and stuff in it, then people who have a long leisure and the mind hunger... they'll give you their time. My characters do what we all do: eat, drink, love, lie, feel...."
    JOHN LECARRÉ, BRITISH AUTHOR OF SPY NOVELS, AT 80

"This is my angel side. Movie making is my devil side. It's adventurous. It's fun. It's why we go to the theater, for excitement, for stirring up emotion and thoughts."
    ANG LEE, FILM DIRECTOR, "CROUCHING TIGER, HIDDEN DRAGON"

ROBERT EDWIN LEE, PLAYWRIGHT — SEE **HENRY DRUMMOND**

"Reality can never catch up with fantasy. 'Cause here's reality; here's fantasy. When reality gets up here, fantasy is already up ahead."
    STAN LEE, CREATOR OF "IRON MAN"

"Sean Penn got me to cry in this scene. If that can happen to the author — I wrote this scene — and rewrote it and rewrote it and if Sean Penn can get tears out of my eyes, then I think we're in a good place here."
    DENNIS LEHANE, AUTHOR, FILM WRITER, "MYSTIC RIVER"

"When I got up and sang at church and saw people get up and clap and it was like, man, this is the life. This is what I want to do."
JOHN LEGEND, GOSPEL SINGER, SONGWRITER, AT 33

"It never occurred to me that I would make a living looking at snowflakes. But when I got into the science, I found it was very interesting and the science led me to do stuff in the lab, so it kinda snowballed. I'm trying to be a snowflake artist. That's one of my goals, to be able to make snowflakes in the lab that look just as nice as the ones outside, maybe even better and more interesting and more elaborate and different because I can control the conditions in the lab."
KENNETH LEIBRECHT, HEAD OF CAL TECH'S PHYSICS DEPARTMENT IN PASADENA, CA (ON MAKING DESIGNER SNOWFLAKES)

Advice to actors: "Take things that scare you, kid, and it'll pay off because you'll learn."
JACK LEMMON (1919-2011) ACTOR

"Imagine!"
JOHN LENNON (1940-1980) SONGWRITER, MUSICIAN, BEATLES

"Six months ago I had no idea I'd be doing any of the things I'm doing now. Not a clue. There's a joy to this, a freedom to this."
JULIAN LENNON, SINGER TURNED PROFESSIONAL PHOTOGRAPHER, AT 47

"Music is a really precious thing. I don't believe in finding a formula that works commercially.... People that paint paintings don't have the gallery owner standing behind them saying, 'Could you paint that a bit more blue because blue is what's selling this year?' I like to experiment and explore with music. That's the joy of the creative process."
ANNIE LENNOX, SINGER, SONGWRITER, MUSICAL ARTIST, AT 52

"I never write from my point of view. Never. I don't want readers ever to be aware of me. I want you to be lost in the book, the same way I get lost when I'm writing it. It all starts with a character; I seldom plot — not until I get into the book. I meet my characters and get to know what they're about and then they kind of point the way."
ELMORE LEONARD, AUTHOR, *GET SHORTY* AND OTHER ACTION BOOKS, AT 72

"Conglomerates don't care if books are wonderful or not — but they better sell.... What they are trying to sell us is a surefire, failsafe, super-commodity print pack called something like: how I lost weight, found God, sold short, and changed my sexual preference after abduction by aliens in the Bermuda Triangle."
  JOHN LEONARD (1938-2008) BOOK AND TV REVIEWER, AT 60

"I'm the king of the street. I can ride between objects that leave me an inch and a half on each side. It's so technical, like a surgeon's hands.... It is a dangerous job. Only the strong survive. I'm cautious, yes, because I want my children to have a father and my wife to have a husband."
  DAVID LEOPOLD, OWNER BICYCLE MESSENGER SERVICE, NYC

"I've been doing this so long (using my butt to direct traffic), that I think they let me get away with it. It's showy; let's face it. But it works."
  TONY LEPORE, DANCING COP IN PROVIDENCE RI, AT 62

"I cried when I wrote that scene, and later when I read it, because of what I did to those children. (I got the idea for the book) when I was in Wal-Mart, and I remember thinking, 'You could live here.'"
  BILLIE LETTS, AUTHOR, *WHERE THE HEART IS*

"I think I've done four- or maybe five-thousand drawings. The hand never stops. When I'm asleep, I have to hold onto it."
  DAVID LEVINE (1926-2009) ARTIST, POLITICAL CARTOONIST, AT 74

"I couldn't find the joy in the work if I worked to somebody else's rhythm, and I just have a very slothful rhythm. I like things that make you grit your teeth. I like tucking my chin in and sorta leaning into the storm. I like that feeling. I like it a lot."
  DANIEL DAY LEWIS, ACTOR, ACTION FILMS

"I'm always the nine-year-old."
  JERRY LEWIS, COMEDIAN, ACTOR

"We had to do it. I think there is some force, and sometimes I call it the spirit of history, that maybe just maybe tracked us down and said, 'This is your time and you must do it. If you don't, who will?'"
  JOHN LEWIS, CIVIL RIGHTS DEMONSTRATOR AT SELMA, ALABAMA IN THE 1960S

"Capitalism's great genius is turning social vices into commercial virtues. It takes people's worst qualities and makes them work for the society."
> MICHAEL LEWIS, AUTHOR, *THE NEW NEW THING*

"All young people should see 'Undefeated'. A great lesson in self-motivation, self-pride, and how losing is just as important as winning."
> RAMSEY LEWIS, JAZZ PIANIST, AT 76

At 38: "I was happy to play classical music; I loved it, but the musical purist types were not the people I wanted to please."
At 68: "People associate me with a certain amount of fantasy. Show business is fantasy. I think you have to take their daily lives – sometimes humdrum lives — and throw in a little bit of pizzaz and sparkle."
> WLADZIU VALENTINO LIBERACE (1919-1987) POPULAR TELEVISION PIANIST, PERFORMER

"We (Mike Stoller and I) never tried to write rock and roll; we were just trying to write good rhythm and blues."
> JEROME "JERRY" LIEBER (1933-2011) SONGWRITER, INDUCTED INTO 1987 ROCK AND ROLL HALL OF FAME, AT 54

"When the material is there and it's ready to go, it will leap off the page at you and you'll just start working.... You see what has happened to them (characters) without being told. That's good writing — when writing allows you (the actor) to actually act. The test of writing a good part: if you start working on it before you finish reading it."
> LAURA LINNEY, ACTOR, FILMS AND TELEVISION, AT 44

"When you make your enemy look ridiculous, you've won."
> JOAN LITTLEWOOD (1914-2002) PLAYWRIGHT

"I knew that there was a sea of young talent that was good if they just had a chance."
> HORACE LEE LOGAN (1916-2002) PERFORMER ON LOUISIANA HAYRIDE RADIO SHOW (1948-58), PROMOTER OF COUNTRY SINGERS (HANK WILLIAMS, JOHNNY CASH, ELVIS PRESLEY)

"An image comes through dreams — comes visually to the ear. Whatever music a person does, ultimately it has to be to heal people; it has to provide a bridge for them to cross out of their hopelessness, out

of their terror, out of their darkness. To me, that is the highest ideal and purpose of music — to heal."
>> **HANNIBAL LOKUMBA**, COMPOSER, TRUMPET PLAYER, MUSICIAN, "AFRICAN PORTRAITS"

"All I know about bands, which is not very much, but I've done it for 60-some years, you better have F-U-N. If you change that, it's over. I would like to be remembered as a teacher. I think *teacher* is the greatest word in the English language, next to *mother*."
>> **JOHNNY LONG** (1943-2000) RETIRED BAND DIRECTOR, AT 85

"I looked like a sex bomb, but I was not. I was very much tortured inside. I was a woman, one hundred percent with problems.... (Acting) is a kind of vacation. But difficult, sometimes, because sometimes you are given things to do that are very very difficult, sometimes. But, it distracts you a little bit."
>> **SOPHIA LOREN**, FILM STAR, AT 75

"A writer has to be somebody who's looking at the world and saying, 'Tell me that again.' You need to try to understand."
>> **BRET LOTT**, AUTHOR, *JEWEL*

"I so enjoy what I do. And that's what I want my audience to see. It's such a God-given gift to me, at my age, to be doing what I'm doing."
>> **DARLENE LOVE**, RHYTHM AND BLUES SINGER, AT 70

"The point is, you can let the past screw with your head for a lifetime, or you can say, 'All we have is right now'."
>> **MIKE LOVE**, FOUNDING MEMBER OF THE BEACH BOYS, AT THE 50TH REUNION, AT 70

"My mother took me, at age 8, to a local production of "Oliver", and it was like a clicked moment... and when I literally saw what I wanted to do with my life, it changed my life.... It's what you do when the phone isn't ringing, how you re-invent yourself, how you keep yourself fresh and engaged and positive."
>> **ROB LOWE**, ACTOR, FILM AND TELEVISION, AT 47

"I'm going back to that studio on Monday and I'm going to play Erica Kane for all she's worth."
>> **SUSAN LUCCI**, TELEVISION ACTOR, UPON WINNING AN EMMY ON HER 19TH NOMINATION, AT 65

"I was chosen. And I have respect for the talent I have been given by God. I love the audience. What else needs to be said? This is the natural progression. I'm doing what I'm supposed to be doing. I'm thrilled to death that I'm being allowed to do it."
    PATTI LUPONE, "ACTOR WHO SINGS" (HER WORDS)

"I ain't about to be nobody else. If I was trying to be somebody else, I'd never made it here."
    LORETTA LYNN, COUNTRY MUSIC SINGER, AUTHOR, AT 76

"Being a hellcat? It's more interesting than being politically correct. I don't like rules. I don't like authority. I don't like people telling me what to do. And I don't like people who like people telling me what to do. When tragedy happens, you have two choices: you live or you die. Thank God, I had music."
    SHELBY LYNNE, SINGER, COUNTRY MUSIC, ROCK, AT 39

"Somebody else decided to sculpt with oleo… and it was a flop."
    NORMA "DUFFY" LYON 1929-2011) IOWA "BUTTER COW LADY" SCULPTOR, AT 74

~M~

"I'm a musical comedy performer who dabbles in spirituality and jewelry. Everything will be all right. Da-ta-da-ta-da-da! I now feel like I have heart knowledge where I can more readily practice acceptance, responsibility, and kindness every day, even when I want to be basically so cranky…. If I didn't hit on that understanding of her (the character I play) and let her be who she wanted to be, it doesn't work."
    SHIRLEY MACLAINE, ACTOR, SINGER, DANCER, AUTHOR

"I wanted to spread the gospel about the great folk art, and that, for me, is exactly what happened. That dream came true for me. I've a lot to do yet, if the Lord spares me."
    PATTY MALONE, GOSPEL SINGER WITH THE CHIEFTANS, DUBLIN, IRELAND, MUSICIANS, AT 73

"I honestly don't know how to make a hit record. I don't know what to do. I just know what feels good to me. And that's all I can do."
    BARRY MANILOW, SINGER, SONGWRITER

"I've introduced the art of mime to the public, the art of silence, the art that speaks to the soul — like music, making comedy and tragedy, involving you, your life, and putting it through the invisible visible, creating characters, space, making a whole show on stage with our life, our dreams, our expectations."
    MARCEL MARCEAU (1923-2007) MIME

"The Chicano experience, our experience, is the American experience. It's as American as macaroni or pizza. 'I am you and you are me and we are all together.' That's it."
    CHEECH MARIN, ACTOR, ART COLLECTOR

"We just love keeping the mystery of it (weaving glass). We love people wondering how it's done."
    ERIC MARKOW, GLASS ARTIST, CHEMICAL ENGINEER
    — SEE **TOM NORRIS**

"Stand up for your rights." (taken from song: "Get Up, Stand Up")
    BOB MARLEY (1945-1981) REGGAE MUSICIAN, SONGWRITER

"I've had this vision for a long time of 'What would God's living room look like?' He'd have these framed pieces of all his prototypes, everything immaculately portrayed, perfectly clean and beautiful. That's what I'm trying to create, something that would look good in God's own living room."
    CHRISOPHER MARLEY, ARTIST (FRAMED WORKS OF BUGS),
    AUTHOR, *PHEROMONE*

"My father (Bob Marley) is more than my father. My father is my inspiration; he's my mentor; he's my hero. When I sing his songs, it's the best I ever sing."
    ZIGGY MARLEY, REGGAE MUSICIAN, AT 41

"It was like this weird tribe of people that come out of nowhere and this whole movement happened. It was really cool."
    BRIT MARLING, FILM PRODUCER, ACTOR, WRITER, AT 27

"There's a pattern. I didn't create this pattern, I just realized that this is how faces are made, a mathematical design for physical beauty, a perfectly proportioned face."
    STEVEN MARQUARDT, MD, COSMETIC SURGEON
    — SEE **RICHARD ALLENBOGAN**

"Don't show off! Those who play for applause, that's all they get. Play for yourself."
> **ELLIS MARSALLIS**, JAZZ MUSICIAN

"Think for yourself; what works best for you? Don't dismiss what you're taught just because you're too lazy to practice. Be optimistic. How you feel about living in the world is who you are! When you're optimistic, the world is always wonderful; when you're pessimistic, you have a bad time. Think like the blues: things are bad, but they'll get better. Look for connections; everything is related.... The myth is the one you keep out and you push down and you kick — that's the one with the moral authority, with the gift. That's as old as night and day, as old as dust, and it's not about black or white. It is not that same story in black and white."
> **WYNTON MARSALLIS**, JAZZ MUSICIAN

At 31: "They ask, 'What are those Cadillacs doing up in your wheat field?' I tell them, 'whatever is my fancy'."
At 73: "Pancakes told me to build it. You know, pancakes talk if you pay attention to their sizzle.... Why not? It's art.... Art is a legalized form of insanity, and I do it very well."
> **STANLEY MARSH 3**, ARTIST, PHILANTHROPIST, OWNER CADILLAC RANCH, AMARILLO TX

"Love is nice. I tried once to blow something up (in a movie). I don't blow things up well; it frightens me... I do two people in a room."
> **GARRY MARSHALL**, TV AND MOVIE DIRECTOR, ACTOR, AT 75

"You have to work hard. But I don't think of it as hard work. That sounded quite poetic, but it's so true."
> **CHRIS MARTIN**, BRITISH ROCK SONGWRITER, SINGER, AT 34

At 57: "Writing for the stage is thrilling and terrifying. When you're sitting in the theater and watching people laughing or listening or crying, you have a hard time denying what you've done.... I need to do it for my heart and soul. I only do it when I'm really really ready.... I just wait and wait and wait until I can't stop myself anymore and it just has to come out.... Art is the best thing humans do — paint these things and write this stuff."
On comedy timing: "Precision in poetry, ballet, or comedy forces a movement and keeps you interested. I learned how to write from doing it.

At 65: "There's finding the idea; there's finding the words for it; then there's finding the exact words for it. That's the great thrill."
> **STEVE MARTIN**, ACTOR, COMEDIAN, AUTHOR, PLAYWRIGHT, SCREENWRITER, PRODUCER, ESSAYIST

"It (building a terrarium) is just something that helps us to cope. It's just calming to think of nature and our roots."
> **TOVAH MARTIN**, TERRARIUM DESIGNER, HORTICULTURIST, AUTHOR, LECTURER

"Is it sad or high-kickin'? It's important in life to make it as high-kickin' as you can."
Q: *How do you want to be remembered?*
A: Preferably alive.
> **GROUCHO MARX** (1890-1977) COMEDIAN, SHOWMAN, FILMS, RADIO, TELEVISION, AT 86

"There's no such thing as too late. That's why they invented death."
> **WALTER MATHAU** (1920-2000) ACTOR, QUOTING HIS CHARACTER CHARLIE JORDON IN "OUT TO SEA"

"Music is a wonderful memory maker. It will take yourself immediately out of yourself, out of the present, and put you where you want to go."
> **JOHNNY MATHIS**, SINGER, AT 71

"Accuracy is not art."
> **HENRI MATISSE** (1869-1954) ARTIST

"We're pretty strange in the whole picture. Not a lot of people sound like us. That's a good thing too. It's good to be a little strange."
> **DAVE MATTHEWS**, DAVE MATTHEWS BAND, FOLK, JAZZ, FUNK, ROCK MUSIC

"I feel useful. If I died tomorrow, I think I've done something that I'm proud of in terms of helping people make the same journey that I made and to make it in good spirits."
> **ARMISTEAD MAUPIN**, AUTHOR *TALES OF THE CITY*, AT 63

"…and when you breakfast on the lawn under the Tuscan sun, any other life is hard to imagine."
> **FRANCES MAYES**, AUTHOR, *UNDER THE TUSCAN SUN*

On inspiration: "It ('Yesterday') came in a dream to me. I woke up one morning and it was there. I thought I'd heard it because it was so complete. The words took a little longer, but the tune was there, complete. You have to believe in magic."

At 63: *On the new album:* "There's a fine line between recklessness and courage. I said to myself, 'I'm going to make a good album'; I gave myself a task, whereas normally you come in... and wonder what's going to happen today.... But on this album I said no, don't stop there, but actually come in the studio with some stuff you're really proud of. And then work this record; don't let anything escape.... One of the things I like about getting older is you can free your emotions more."

On audiences: "The audiences are so great, and that's what it is. It's the only point in your career when you actually get all these people sitting there, feeding back this thing that you just felt. And it's pretty powerful. It really is. It hooks you. There's a connection, I can't help it, and I don't want to look away from it. I like it. And this is great, like real!"

At 67: Looking back, I think we (John Lennon and McCartney) wrote close to 300 songs. Every day we wrote a song; we would spend probably three hours; we wrote one. We must have liked it or something."

  PAUL MCCARTNEY, THE BEATTLES, SONGWRITER, SINGER, MUSICIAN
  SEE — **JOHN LENNON**

Darryl: I love your song; it really helped me,"
Sarah: Thank you for telling me that, Darryl, because that's what music is supposed to do."
Darryl: I learned that I am who I am, Sarah, and I was already Darryl. Nothing really changes. I just got stuff that was added onto me that makes me complete."

  DARRYL MCDANIELS, HIP-HOP RAPPER, IN CONVERSATION WITH **SARAH MCLAUGHLIN**, SINGER

"You don't know your age, at least I don't, until you read it in a newspaper... and you're like 'oh, that's me', and this is the journey... getting older and embracing it, because if you fight it, that's when the suffering starts."

  DYLAN MCDERMOTT, TELEVISION ACTOR, AT 50

"I was a little girl with a pot belly and Afro puffs, hyperactive and overdramatic, and I found the theater and I found my home. I found a place to express myself and I was so grateful at the age of 9. And to think the theater would be so good to me… is mind blowing."
    AUDRA MCDONALD, STAGE ACTRESS AFTER WINNING BEST ACTRESS TONY AWARD (2012), AT 41

"The white man signs my checks. I write what I want to write and they run what they want to run."
    AARON MCGRUDER, CARTOONIST, "THE BOONDOCKS"

"It's a grind, but it's a great feeling at the end of it, like you've brought a project to life all by yourself."
    WAYNE MCKENDLISH, BUILDS TOOTHPICK STRUCTURES

"I wanted something nobody else had. Something different. I guess because I'm different."
    RON MCLARTY, ACTOR, AUTHOR, READER OF AUDIO BOOKS
    — SEE **JIM DALE**

SARAH MCLAUGHLIN — SEE **DARRYL MCDANIELS**

"It's meant to be vague because it's meant to be a dream. It's a cautionary tale written to America about what happens when the spirit goes out of something, and when you start to put commercial things ahead of beauty and poetry and literature."
    DON MCLEAN, SINGER, SONGWRITER "AMERICAN PIE", AT 61

"I have no ideas until I sit down at the machine. I do it at the same time every day. And whatever process I have starts when I hit the keys and stops when I get to the end of five pages."
    LARRY MCMURTRY, SCREENWRITER

"When you write, you're not the person you usually are."
    KATE MEDINA, EDITOR

"Whenever I start writing songs, I always have a vague notion. In 'Freedom's Road', I wrote 'Sometimes you wonder what kind of freedom you're talkin'… and when I wrote that line I thought, 'that's what this record is going to be about.' That one line was a kind of catalyst to the whole album."
    JOHN MELLENCAMP, MUSICIAN, SONGWRITER

"I know of no human being who has a better time than an eager and energetic young reporter."
   H. L. MENCKEN (1880-1956) AUTHOR, HISTORIAN

"Honestly, the best award is going to the first day of rehearsal and everybody's there and they're excited, and there's a joy and you've created something that is real. Infectious, amazing."
   ALAN MENKEN, OSCAR WINNING SONGWRITER FOR FILMS AND STAGE, AT 62

"I noticed that many of my lyrics referred to 'like a child at play', memories of childhood. I came to New York to be an actor, telling myself, 'I'm going to New York and make my fortune, a Horatio Alger story'."
   JOHNNY MERCER (1909-1976) SONGWRITER, LYRICIST (500+ SONGS)

"Everything you do has to have passion or what is the point of doing anything? If you are in love, it has to be a passionate love. If you are eating something, it has to be a passionate meal. If you are doing something — making a movie — it has to be a passionate film, or otherwise, why do anything?"
   ISMAEL MERCHANT, FILM PRODUCER, "THE GOLDEN BOWL"

"I'm not writing that poem for anybody, including me. I'm writing it because I want to write that poem."
   WILLIAM STANLEY MERWIN, 17TH U.S. POET LAUREATE, AT 83

"I never dreamed of being a writer… I had this completely amazing dream that was about first love and all of the emotions that it'd been a long time since I thought about. I wrote it down and made my dream into a real existence, and I was hooked on writing from that day."
   STEPHENIE MEYER, AUTHOR, "TWILIGHT" SERIES

"There has to be a piece of what I think is truth to it. So 'I don't have a huge imagination' is what I'm saying."
   NANCY MEYERS, FILM WRITER, DIRECTOR, AT 60

"Cherish forever what makes you unique, 'cuz you're really a yawn if it goes."
   BETTE MIDLER, ENTERTAINER, PERFORMER, ACTOR, SINGER, GRAMMY WINNER

"The program is to teach children about empathy and compassion, something very important for the future of America, for the future of the world. And so to have that empathy and compassion toward animals, we can then practice that with humans."
  CESAR MILAN, DOG WHISPERER, FOUNDER, MUTT-I-GREE PROGRAM, AT 41

"We are born afraid. How we deal with fear is up to us. Everyone feels persecuted. Yet, you can't find anyone who persecutes others.... Forgive others — those you fear (hate). Forgive yourself. Lighten up! Stop blaming 'them' and stop living in fear.... Tragedy is forward motion leading to a dreaded action. Now we have flow that rushes along without shape or direction. Something happened. Our country has had two acts of tragedy. Then something happened to redirect our attention. No longer do we need direction, just movement."
On Longevity of Success: "Keep your cholesterol low."
On Making a Difference: "It's hard to imagine, but I do think that somehow a play can put a drop of acid in the water and it spreads through the system and washes away a lot of rust."
  ARTHUR MILLER (1915-2005) AUTHOR/PLAYWRIGHT

"I see myself as kind of a journeyman who's worked hard and has written some good songs that people enjoy and I've done really good concerts, and I've delivered a lot of value to my audience. I want to take the guitar off. I'm done. Now I'm just me again. I think I'm pretty much just a normal guy. Really. Sometimes if I go into town and walk into a bar and people start bugging me, I can go, 'O Jeez, I forgot!'"
  STEVE MILLER, CLASSIC ROCK MUSICIAN, AT 50

"The needs of fiction consist of writers doing terrible things to characters, (things) that they would never wish on anyone... Jo is an aggravating character, and if readers are aggravated, imagine how it was to live inside her head for two years."
  SUE MILLER, AUTHOR, *WHILE I WAS GONE*

"If I'm learning the lyrics, I have the picture of the woman. What is she showing, hiding? What happened to her before she started to sing? Why is she singing this song? What color carpet is in living room? To the finest detail, because details count. They're the secrets in great singers' eyes. All great singers have them. Make sure you have a secret."
  LIZA MINNELLI, SINGER, ACTOR

"Pure feeling!"
  SUSAN MINOT, AUTHOR, *EVENING*, AND *RAPTURE*

Q: *Where did you get the idea?*
A: "I dreamed it in order. I knew the names of the people and I knew what happened."
  JACQUELYN MITCHARD, AUTHOR, *DEEP END OF THE OCEAN*

As a child: "I want to be famous in some way, artist, writer, soldier, prizefighter, anything for the thrills."
At 38. after her book was made into a movie: "I wasn't cut out to be a celebrity; I don't like it worth a damn."
  MARGARET MITCHELL (1900-1949) AUTHOR, *GONE WITH THE WIND*

Comment by David Edelstein: "Like a child, Miyazaki still builds castles in his imagination. No matter how outlandish his plots, the feelings are real. No matter how surreal his settings, you feel you can disappear in them. Miyazaki maps our inner landscapes and leaves us astonished."
  HAYAO MIYAZAKI, JAPANESE DIRECTOR, ANIMATION "HOWL'S MOVING CASTLE", AT 64

"I'm still learning… each one (guitar) is like a performance."
  JOHN MONTELEONE, GUITAR MAKER, AT 64

"I was meant to be a musician who speaks his mind about social justice issues.… There's a component of music, something that when you get the right combination of rhythm, melody, and the right lyrical couplet, that feels like truth in the reptile brain."
  TOM MORELLA, "THE NIGHT WATCHMAN", MUSICIAN, ARTIST, POLITICIAN, ACTIVIST, AT 47

"A detail at a time, a sentence at a time, an image at a time. You have to put down enough to make it real."
  ROBERT MORGAN, AUTHOR, *GAP CREEK*

"It (my home) is my sanctuary. I'm a sensitive person inside a famous person's body. So, this backyard is where I rest and where I rejuvenate to the point where I can then go out.… The dangling brass ring that all will be well and peaceful when you're famous, I came to find out personally that it's not."
  ALANIS MORISSETTE, SINGER, SONGWRITER, MUSICIAN, AT 34

"So what I had to do was start out with an idea which would be acceptable to the sensitivities of young people, which is why it's told through the eyes of a horse — because the child can access that much more readily."
>   **MICHAEL MORPURGO**, AUTHOR, YOUNG ADULT NOVEL, *WAR HORSE*, AT 68

"Trudging up the Broadway ranks, that was my dream as a child, to be on Broadway. When your dreams come true, you have to make new dreams."
>   **MATTHEW MORRISON**, ACTOR, SINGER, DANCER, MUSICAL THEATER AND TELEVISION, AT 32

"You know, you can taste a book when you can turn a page and see it, turn the words over in your mouth, and hear it and feel as though you've been someplace. When you see only appearance, you see nothing. You need to look past the appearance. Everyone deserves to be loved, validated."
About *Song of Solomon*: "If you won't feel the pain, you can't feel the joy. What do you *have* to do — or else you'll die? I feel very comfortable with my flaws — and with my gifts. Turn up the volume of your life. Life is big!.... A novel has layers: plots and something going on with the characters... and something under that... and something under that... so many layers.
At 69: About *The Bluest Eye*: "I still feel totally entangled emotionally. I am very vulnerable to them, the characters... I write because I'm compelled to. I have to! I write for myself. If there's an audience, it's the characters. I know I'd keep writing, even if no one reads my work."
>   **TONI MORRISON**, AUTHOR, RECEIVED THE NOBEL PRIZE IN LITERATURE IN 1993, MEDAL OF FREEDOM IN 2012, AT 71

"My music has lived a public life; I haven't.... When it doesn't come, you just have to make it happen. You take a blank piece of paper and wait, until something comes. I go to a place that is like a light trance. If the musicians can follow me, it's easy; if they give me the right support, then I can do anything, go anywhere."
>   **VAN MORRISON**, IRISH SINGER, SONGWRITER

"A real gambler would choose life over death."
>   **DCI MORSE**, FICTIONAL CHARACTER DEVISED BY AUTHOR COLIN DEXTER IN PBS MYSTERY SERIES, 1987-2000

"You really have to believe in yourself; you really do. If you feel strong enough, you should pursue it. And don't let anything or anyone hold you back."
    MARI MOVAS, DOLL MAKER

WOLFGANG AMADEUS MOZART — SEE BRIAN SELZER

"If you want something to happen, you can make it happen. That's what we teach the kids.... All of us came to this country for a better life, for a fresh start, to live the American dream, and there's not many places you can start fresh and accomplish whatever you want and be whomever you want."
    LUMA MUFLEH, FOUNDER FUGEES FAMILY INC., AT 36

"I've got work on seven continents.... I have a touch that no one else possesses... pushing impossibilities."
    RAY MURPHY, "FATHER OF CHAINSAW ART", FROM MAINE, AT 69

"Time, don't run out on me / Gotta get back where we used to be / Time, don't run out on me!"
    ANN MURRAY, SINGER, SONGWRITER

On improvisation: "Agree and... yes and... heighten and explore."
    MIKE MYERS, ACTOR, COMEDIAN, SCREENWRITER, FILM PRODUCER, CAST MEMBER "SATURDAY NIGHT LIVE"

~N~

"My quilts are to be looked at. I don't put one on my bed. They're all on my walls in my apartment. It gives me so many possibilities. That's what looking in a kaleidoscope has taught me, that there are so many possibilities. Whenever I don't quite know where to go with a quilt, I very often come over and look at this (kaleidoscope)."
    PAULA NADELSTERN, QUILT ARTIST, USING KALEIDOSCOPE DESIGNS

"Where there's a monster, there's a miracle."
    FREDERIC OGDEN NASH (1902-1971) POET, HUMORIST

…Your Song / 95

Who is she? She dared to become a painter at a time when women were given short shrift in the arts, a nonconformist who created "figurative painting". She showed the human face and form in a way that was not photographically realistic. She became adept at showing the child in the grownup, the grownup in the child.

At 60 she became a "star", painting Ann Miller for the cover of *Time*, Andy Warhol recovering from a stab wound, and many of the '60s Bohemian glitterati. She appeared often on the "Johnny Carson Show" and was honored by President Jimmy Carter. In 1980, at the age of 80, she painted a self portrait — nude. Who is she?

ALICE NEEL (1900-1984) ARTIST

"I've seen a lot and done a lot. And what have I learned? I've learned that it's better to take it easy. Not rush anything. Patience. I've learned that."

WILLY NELSON, COUNTRY SINGER, MUSICIAN

"When I was thirteen and going 'that's me up on that stage', I had just found myself. (Bob Fossey) kinda showed me who I am as an artist and as a performer. He saw me. That's what we look for in life, people who see us. That brings out the best you are."

BEBE NEUWIRTH, ACTOR, SINGER, PERFORMER ON STAGE, TELEVISION, AND FILM, AT 51

"We started to add more types of dancing… not just tap dancing, because we work with the whole body. We use our hands, everything, the head all the way down to our feet."

NICHOLAS BROTHERS, HAROLD (1917-2001) AND **FAYART** (1914-2006) VAUDEVILLE/CLUB DANCERS

About van Gogh's painting, "Fields": "A cloud doesn't look like that; the sky doesn't look like that, but van Gogh's experience of the sky looks that way. Despite his occasional bouts of mental illness, van Gogh was anything but mad. He was well read, of the world, and absolutely maniacally focused on what he was creating. But that's not madness. That's genius."

LARRY NICHOLS, CURATOR, TOLEDO MUSEUM OF ART, ABOUT THE DUTCH MASTERS IN TOLEDO COLLECTION ON THE 150TH ANNIVERSARY OF **VINCENT VAN GOGH'S** BIRTH

"She shifts her soul slightly and forever changes the chemistry."

MIKE NICHOLS, DIRECTOR/PRODUCER, ABOUT **MERYL STREEP**

"My life is fantastic. I never wanted to be a solo star; being in an elite rock and roll band was way better than being a solo star. I'm really an entertainer. I'm not just a rock and roll star; I would be entertaining even if we didn't make it, because I love to perform."
> **STEVIE NICKS**, SINGER, MUSICIAN, FLEETWOOD MAC, AT 57

"Singing is the best way to tell a story. It's an abstraction; it's a beauty; it's a long line of things, and you perceive the whole story without ever a word sometimes."
> **MARNI (MARGARET) NIXON**, SINGER, DUBBED MUSIC FOR FILM STARS (DEBORAH KERR, NATALIE WOOD, AUDREY HEPBURN)

"I'm in a lonely spot between two worlds. That chapter (life in the U.S.) did not close when I married and moved to the Middle East to live. No. Nothing has closed. There are always opportunities and challenges in front of us that we need to address."
> **QUEEN NOOR** (LISA HAJEEB HALABY), AUTHOR, WIDOW OF KING HUSSEIN OF JORDAN

"When we look at our process (for glass weaving), we always want to push it, and we always want to go a bit further and take it beyond the actual fabric into the sculptural."
> **TOM NORRIS**, GLASS ARTIST, BIOLOGIST
> — SEE **ERIC MARKOW**

"I like to play with architecture. It's my favorite game. I think architecture has to be a gift."
> **JEAN NOUVELLE**, FRENCH ARCHITECT, WINNER PRITZKER PRIZE 2008, AT 65

~O~

"We have to decide we are goddess. It's probably illusion. But if I have illusion, I'd like to have a good illusion, not a bad one. Creating art is not terribly important, but finding myself through creating art is more important to me.... A lot of people can do a better gardening; a lot of people can do better teaching, but I have a thing I wanted to say that probably nobody can do."
> **MAYUMI ODA**, JAPANESE ARTIST, EXTENSIVE WORK WITH GODDESS IMAGERY, AT 60

"I had to go along with the horrible things that happened to this little family. Sometimes it was very disturbing and hard to write certain scenes."
    TAWNI O'DELL, AUTHOR, *BACK ROADS*

"When you yell, nobody hears you. The best communicators have to be live and present themselves in a peaceful manner, and that's going to be a lifelong quest of mine, because I get so angry at the things that I think are unjust."
    ROSIE O'DONNELL, ACTOR, COMEDIAN, AUTHOR, TALK SHOW HOST, PERFORMER, AT 47

"I sat on the headland and looked out on the world. I'm pioneering how to get old. I don't know what's going to become of me. I'll end up in the west of Ireland in an old tweed coat held together with a bit of string, and broken Wellington boots, and I'll have 59 dogs and a hundred cats, and I'll drink just a little bit too much and look back on these glory days. Now what else can I do but look after my teeth, listen to all the music I can, and keep going. What can I do when everything is so various and so beyond me but cling on and thank the god I don't believe in for the miracles showered on me."
    NUALA O'FAOLLAIN (1940-2008) IRISH JOURNALIST, TV PRODUCER, TEACHER, AUTHOR, *ARE YOU SOMEBODY?* AT 58

"I thought someone could tell me how to paint a landscape, but I couldn't find anyone. They could tell me how they paint their landscape, but they couldn't tell me how to paint mine. They said, 'What do you think you're doing? The men haven't done very well with it (painting the city of New York); what do you think you'll do with it?'"
    GEORGIA O'KEEFE (1887-1986) ARTIST

"I've got to do a lot of things in my life, but this (book) was one of the few things I knew… it must be love. There was no choice; it must be done, and I'm so happy I got to do it."
    TODD OLDHAM, DESIGNER, ARTIST, AUTHOR, *CHARLEY HARPER*

"The writer's life consists of transmitting reality, making it legible, setting it down on the page.… Don't ever let anyone set your boundaries. Never underestimate the power of a dream, of imagination, and passion, and what any person is capable of

achieving... ordinary individuals like you and me... with flaws, weaknesses, limitations, fears and prejudices that had to be overcome. There is no simple way to explain a life. Only life does that."
>   **CHARLES OSGOOD**, AUTHOR, POET, TELEVISION AND RADIO PERSONALITY, AT 64

"Life is not for sissies. Love isn't easy. It's not easy if you find it; it's not easy if you don't find it. It's not easy if you find it but it doesn't work out. It's hard in a very specific way for everyone."
>   **DIANA OSSANA**, AUTHOR

"It distresses us to return work that is not perfect."
>   **PETER O'TOOLE**, HIS CHOSEN EPITAPH (FROM A DRY CLEANER'S NOTE)

"Me and Queen Latifah used to be the same person, and then somewhere along the line she got much bigger than me. She became a corporation and a company; she became a brand."
>   **DANA OWENS**, ACTOR, SINGER

~P~

At 11: "When my grandfather said, 'I like country music,' I said, 'By golly, that's what I like.'"
At 39: "One of the things he (grandfather) told me: 'You learn to play with this guitar and you'll never be alone.' He's right about that. That's the beauty of country music: nothing is off limits."
>   **BRAD PAISLEY**, COUNTRY MUSIC STAR

This successful author never had a single rejection slip throughout the writing of his 36-plus novels. He'd send a one-line query: "Would you care to publish this? Sincerely Robert B. Parker."
On his career: "It's all been easy."
>   **ROBERT B. PARKER** (1932-2010) AUTHOR OF SPENSER DETECTIVE STORIES

"Being a writer is like having an illness, and the pain is alleviated by scratching on a piece of paper. Ideas are like an airborne virus that goes down your throat, enters your brain and only writing will relieve it."
SUZAN-LORI PARKS, PLAYWRIGHT, "TOPDOG/UNDERDOG", WINNER OF 2002 PULITZER PRIZE FOR DRAMA

"I never thought of it (aging).... It's kind of bad how it seeps into you. (In acting) you're a completely different person. I could not do in real life what I do on stage. It's amazing when you're in a position where you can't ask for anything more; you have it. I feel so lucky, so blessed."
ESTELLE PARSONS, ACTOR, AT "80-PLUS"

"Here's why I don't worry. I will find a way to act, whether it's in my mother's back yard making my sister put on a show with me... in what form... that's where I'll end up being."
JIM PARSONS, ACTOR, TELEVISION AND STAGE, AT 38

At 86: "I get out of bed just because it's Monday. I love to play. I love to entertain. I love to make people laugh, love to make people happy. That's what keeps me going.... You can play a million notes — or you can play one. Can you put it right there and say, 'Goodness, that's it!'?"
On his invention: "Just to be able to put my name on an idea and have it come true — there's a lot of dreams come true in my lifetime."
At 94: "This block of wood, that is the key to the whole thing (solid body electric guitar). A speaker from a telephone, a door hinge, a string, and a block of wood. There it is; it's so simple."
LES PAUL (1915-2009) MUSICIAN, CREATOR OF SOLID ELECTRIC GUITAR

"In order to have a good idea, you have to have lots of ideas."
LINUS PAULING (1901-1994) PEACE ACTIVIST, AUTHOR, CHEMIST

"We don't beat The Reaper by living longer. We beat The Reaper by living well, and living fully.... I don't know how not to have fun. I'm dying and I'm having fun, and I'm going to keep having fun every day I have left. If you lead your life the right way, the karma will take care of itself — the dreams will come to you."
RANDY PAUSCH (1961-2008) AUTHOR, LECTURER, COMPUTER SCIENCE PROFESSOR AT CARNEGIE MELLON UNIV., PRESENTED "THE LAST LECTURE" AND TURNED IT INTO A BOOK.

"I think I reached out to that audience to try to make contact with them, try to make friends with them, and to tell them a story that I wanted to tell."
      GREGORY PECK (1916-2003) ACTOR, AT 70

At 90: "Have a passion. And be always looking ahead."
      GILES PELLERAN (1906-1998) USC FOOTBALL FAN, DIED AT AGE 91 WHILE ATTENDING HIS 797TH USC FOOTBALL GAME

"They were saying things like 'who said she could run?' and it's like, oh-kay. I didn't come here about me. I came here about policy and the issues."
      NANCY PELOSI, FIRST WOMAN SPEAKER OF THE HOUSE OF REPRESENTATIVES, U.S. CONGRESS, AT 70

"Drawing pushes you toward obsession. Every line is a word. Every line is a selection of ten possible lines you can draw, and you choose. I think it's very similar to the way writers treat words. If you use too many, you've lost the person who is listening or reading you. I intend to be obsessive at times… but I say it's cool… who cares?… obsession is good."
      MATTEO PERICOLI, ITALIAN ARCHITECT, ARTIST, CREATOR OF *WINDOW VIEWS* (FROM WINDOWS OF NEW YORK CELEBRITIES)

"You can't just change your dress, or just change your hair; that can't just be the basis of success. It has to spawn from something more powerful. It has to spawn from talent."
      KATY PERRY, POP SINGER, AT 25

"It was not difficult. I just had to grab the pole and get on that wire. It's not difficult, but it was the most difficult thing in the world to do, of course. I was not gambling my life. I was doing something much more beautiful. I was carrying my life across. I wanted to use the wire as a stage, and I wanted to do something… profound or something inspiring…. I am going through life looking for interesting challenges."
      PHILIPPE PETIT, THE MAN ON THE WIRE BETWEEN THE TWIN TOWERS (NEW YORK), AT 60

"I think if you're going out to, say, 30,000 people and you don't get nervous, there's something not plugged in."
      TOM PETTY, ROCK STAR, MUSICIAN, WITH THE HEARTBREAKERS, AT 59

"Non, je ne regrette rien." (I regret nothing.)
>   ÉDITH PIAF (1915-1963) FRENCH CABARET SINGER

"It has been my motto to never stop believing in myself... all the hardships I've gone through, I never stopped believing that some day there is something magical that will happen in my life."
>   ARNEL PINEDA, LEAD SINGER JOURNEY, HEADS FOUNDATION FOR FILIPINO CHILDREN, AT 43
>   — SEE JONATHAN KANE

PINK MARTINI — SEE THOMAS LAUDERDALE AND CHINA FORBES

"Creativity is the ability to give the world something it didn't know it was missing, to create something fundamentally new."
>   DANIEL PINK, AUTHOR

"We don't remember the words we hear, but we do remember the ideas. The purpose of language is to supply the content of thoughts: persuading, convincing, influencing, winning others.... Artists create from visual images, then seek words to express them... experience comes first."
>   STEVEN PINKER, LINGUISTICS PROFESSOR M.I.T., AUTHOR

"I'm now the senior level of my family. I'm the elder... and that means... that I'm... the next to go out. I just hope I can leave something good for them."
>   BILL PINKNEY, AUTHOR, *As Long As It Takes*, THE FIFTH AMERICAN TO SAIL SOLO AROUND THE WORLD; TRACED THE MIDDLE-ATLANTIC ROUTE OF THE SLAVE SHIPS AS CAPTAIN OF ARMISTAD, REPLICA OF THE INFAMOUS SLAVE SHIP, AT 73

"I have this reflex, for better or worse, that makes me do the opposite of what I'm supposed to do. Sometimes it serves me well; sometimes it hasn't."
>   BRAD PITT, FILM ACTOR, AT 48

"What was I afraid of? Not being good enough. I don't know who that guy was. Honestly. Because it all changes. That's what I live for — musical stimulation and change. What matters is getting new."
>   ROBERT PLANT, LED ZEPPELIN, COUNTRY DUO MUSICIAN WITH ALISON KRAUSS

"You feel them (a live audience). That's the ticket. It's alive; it's a buzz. I never get tired of walking out of the wings."
    CHRISTOPHER PLUMMER, CANADIAN ACTOR, AT 82

"There's something very sensual, exciting, about touching the dough, working the dough."
    APOLLONIA POILÂNE, OPERATES HER FATHER'S PAIN POILÂNE IN PARIS, AT 26

"The secret is simplicity, most of the time, to make it simple. When you work it (dough) with your hands, you give it something of yourself."
    LIONEL POILÂNE (1945-2002) PARISIAN BAKER, FOUNDER OF PAIN POILÂNE

"The characteristics of an explorer: curiosity and passion about some thing, some place, some people; an open mind. You have to be able to listen to what's being said, look at what you see. And an enormous amount of patience. Explorers are people who have a passion about life, and are often ahead of their time. We all can be explorers."
    MILBERRY POLK, EXPLORER, RECREATED ALEXANDER THE GREAT'S TREK ACROSS THE WESTERN DESERT TO EGYPT

"I have a desire to get inside and dig deeper and deeper into what it means to be a human being."
    SIDNEY POLLACK, MOVIE DIRECTOR,

"The good thing when people knock you down is that, when someone says 'You can't do that', I just want to be like 'Yes, I can. Watch me.'"
    NATALIE PORTMAN, FILM ACTOR, AT 29

"You take the hot dog and you throw it so it spins end over end. It is so important that you don't start taking yourself too seriously."
    P. STEPHAN POTTER, LAWYER, "THE HOT DOG MAN" AT U. OF NEBRASKA STADIUM FROM 1964-2000, AT 67

"The book was like leeched out of me. I didn't know what it was. I just knew that I had been a witness to something that very few people are going to see close up and I needed to speak out, to talk, to write — just to take people there. That's all I set out to do."
    SISTER HELEN PREJEAN, CSJ, AUTHOR OF *DEAD MAN WALKING* (BOOK, MOVIE, OPERA) THAT OFFERED AN EYEWITNESS ACCOUNT OF THE DEATH PENALTY IN THE U.S.

"I'm going to be very famous someday."
>   ELVIS PRESLEY (1934-1976), SINGER, AT 22

"Every day I do something, paint or draw."
>   WILLIS PYLE, LONGTIME ANIMATOR FOR DISNEY FILMS, AT 95

~Q~

QUEEN LATIFAH — SEE DANA OWENS

"The curse of writing: no matter how audacious, it has probably happened somewhere to somebody."
>   ANNA QUINDLEN, AUTHOR, *BLACK AND BLUE*

~R~

"Everything that happens to me the rest of my life, I owe to those films (Harry Potter). But I feel it's given me the grounding in a career that people only wish for. And I want to make the most of the opportunity."
>   DANIEL RADCLIFFE, BRITISH ACTOR, AT 21

"The only thing you ever have to concern yourself with is your own life and how to live every minute of it so long as you're alive."
>   GILDA RADNER (1946-1989) TELEVISION PERFORMER, COMEDIAN

"It's about how to dream and that is why we love it."
>   HOWELL RAINES, AUTHOR, ABOUT THE THIRD MOST REPRINTED BOOK PROBABLY IN THE WORLD (*THE COMPLEAT ANGLER*, BY IZAAK WALTON). [FYI: THE OTHER TWO BOOKS ARE *THE BIBLE* AND JOHN BUNYAN'S *PILGRIM'S PROGRESS*.]

"I tend to sing best about the places that rub. You know, I'm not a real sunny happy singer.... I can't compromise. I gotta sing the songs that mean a lot to me, and I can't do something that's false."
>   BONNIE RAITT, GRAMMY WINNING SINGER, AT 56

"I'm going to do what I have to do in order to get back to the people who are important to me."
>   **ARON RALSTON**, MOTIVATIONAL SPEAKER, SURVIVOR OF 127 HOURS "BETWEEN A ROCK AND A HARD PLACE", AT 35

MARTIN RAMIREZ (1895-1963) ARTIST — SEE **WAYNE THIBAULT**

RANKIN — SEE **JOHN RANKIN WADDELL**

"There are so many more interesting ways to be than right."
>   **ROBERT RAUSCHENBERG**, ARTIST

"Work to succeed. Trust but verify."
>   **RONALD WILSON REAGAN** (1911-2010) 40TH U.S. PRESIDENT, ACTOR

"You're gonna die anyway. Make a difference!"
>   **BERNICE JOHNSON REAGON**, SINGER, SONG TALKER, MUSICIAN, SANG WITH SWEET HONEY IN THE ROCK

"What keeps me going is the idea that if you can do more, you should."
>   **ROBERT REDFORD**, ACTOR, DIRECTOR, FOUNDER OF SUNDANCE FILM FESTIVAL, AT 70

On dancing in the movie, "Isadora": "They (Terry Juveniles) did routines, dance routines, acrobatics, and tap dances…. That was my ambition. I didn't want to be an actress; I wanted to be a Terry Juvenile."

On reviews: "You can't be striving to please; you have to be striving to get at the heart of the matter."
>   **VANESSA REDGRAVE**, ACTOR, RECIPIENT OF TONYS, EMMYS, ACADEMY AWARDS, AT 70

"Check into your own heart; check into your own mind, and write about that, and you won't fail. If you have talent, if you can't spell, it doesn't matter. If you can put down what you're feeling and thinking, what you're examining in life, and what is influencing you, and you say how you really feel about it (not how you think somebody else would like to hear you feel about it, you'll catch everybody."
>   **CARL REINER**, ON RECEIVING THE MARK TWAIN COMEDY AWARD, AT 78

"My philosophy is: give the audience the best seat in the house. I don't like a lot of tricks and gimmicks to make it work. I make movies about people that live on earth. Nobody gets exploded; nobody is running around chasing anything."
 ROB REINER, FILM MAKER, ACTOR, DIRECTOR, AT 63

CHARLES REINHART — SEE **CHEN WAI**

"I don't consider myself bossy, but I do know what I want. I have a gut feeling about a piece of material, but I've never envisioned myself as the director on top of the hill with the megaphone, screaming at a thousand extras."
 JASON REITMAN, FILM DIRECTOR, AT 30

On the day he died: "I think I'm beginning to know something about painting."
 PIERRE AUGUST RENOIR (1841-1919) FRENCH ARTIST, AT 78

"You have to go your own way. If you don't lead, no one will follow. I didn't set out to be number one. I don't think about the competition; I only think about our reader, what will interest our reader. You have to be aware of the times and sort of tune in to things."
 PAIGE RENSE, EDITOR-IN-CHIEF *ARCHITECTURAL DIGEST*, AT 74

"Retirement? From performing, no! Life will retire you. What's more fun than making people laugh, seeing a smile, having them greet you as if they know you, like an old friend, being able to sing for them, dance, move, do impressions, just have a general good time? I love to perform. I've been performing 60 years, so why stop doing what you really love to do the best of all?"
 DEBBIE REYNOLDS, ACTOR, SINGER, DANCER, AUTHOR, AT 79

"I didn't know James would die. I had a nervous breakdown when it happened. I never know what will happen (to the characters)."
 SHERI REYNOLDS, AUTHOR, *THE RAPTURE OF CANAAN*

"I stumbled on the idea of writing from the point of view of the vampire, like an interview with a vampire. The vampire is the perfect metaphor for the way I felt… like a lost person, a person in the dark, a person who was trying to find meaning in life, trying to find a context."
 ANNE RICE, AUTHOR VAMPIRE STORIES

"At 45, you put your arm into your sleeve and your mother's hand comes out."
      ADRIENNE RICH (FROM MARIE BRENNER'S "GREAT DAMES")

"The riffs pop off the fingers, more than the head…. (The mythical Keith) is on a ball and chain. His image carries a long shadow. I love the guy dearly, but I'm still trying to find out who the hell he is."
      KEITH RICHARDS, GUITARIST, SONGWRITER, WITH ROLLING STONES, AT 66

"When you say you want to be famous, what comes with that is the survival of it. *Famous* looks simple, but it consumes you. The only thing I can deliver that's different is I sound like Lionel Richie. Can't change that sound."
      LIONEL RICHIE, R & B SINGER, SONGWRITER, WINNER OF OSCAR AND MANY GRAMMYS, AT 60

"You can't make up (wrong doing). There are some things you gotta do in life that's wrong and you'll never make up for it."
      WILBERT RIDEAU, PRISON REFORMER, AUTHOR, PAROLED AFTER 44 YEARS IN PRISON, AT 68

"I hope the people cry and laugh and dance and whatever they are feeling, but I want to touch them. That's the most important thing about my making music — to touch the people."
      ANDRÉ RIEU, DUTCH VIOLINIST AND ORCHESTRA CONDUCTOR, AT 62

"When you're a teenager, you don't want to be normal. You want to be extraordinary…. Everyone else can turn 40; I'm Molly Ringwald; I'm so associated with being young and with being a teenager, I can't turn 40."
      MOLLY RINGWALD, ACTOR, SINGER, AUTHOR, TEENAGER PLAYING-EVERY-TEEN, AT 43

Q: What do you get out of tap dancing?
A: "Oh my gosh, everything. Eighty percent (of students, average age 60) never tapped before. They've taken their first tap sound with me."
      VICKI G. RIORDAN, FOUNDER, DIRECTOR "TAP PUPS" TAP DANCING SCHOOL FOR GROWNUPS, AUTHOR *ENCORE PERFORMANCE*

"I can have a given situation set up, but it's catching that moment, allowing them to be themselves and capturing something that's special."
>   **HERB RITTS** (1952-2002) CELEBRITY PHOTOGRAPHER, AT 48

"If you're funny, you can be anything. I learned that you go through any door that opens. Nothing is off limits. If it's terrible and you laugh about it, it's OK."
>   **JOAN RIVERS**, COMEDIAN, ACTOR, TELEVISION PERSONALITY, AT 77

"The artist must elect to fight for freedom or slavery. I have made my choice; I had no alternative. 'There is a balm in Gilead to heal the sin sick soul.'"
>   **PAUL ROBESON** (1895-1976) SINGER ON STAGE AND IN FILMS

"I take my fun very seriously. A play is supposed to be fun... it's called a *play*. Any kid can tell you that any kind of play, whether it's on stage, on the baseball diamond, or in the garage building model airplanes, if it isn't fun, if it isn't taken seriously, focus makes for fun. Show Director James Lupine repeated one piece of advice: 'Have fun,' he said. Advice I take very seriously."
>   **MO (MAURICE) ROCCA**, COMMENTATOR "CBS SUNDAY MORNING", COMEDIAN, ACTOR

"My paintings are like *ideas* of those landscapes. If I paint a mountain top, it's not really a mountain top; it's an *idea* of a mountain top."
>   **ED ROCHE**, ARTIST, PUBLISHED *ON THE ROAD*, AT 73

"You've got to be really good to last. You're not going to get by just on being popular.... Being rich is not about having a lot of money; being rich is having lots of options."
>   **CHRIS ROCK**, COMEDIAN, ACTOR, STAGE, AND FILMS, AT 46

"If people have the opportunity to look at a work of art from above, they have perspective. They (sculptures) should be there for 100–200 years. My view of history and time is very long. So really, they're only a moment in time, and they're not large structures either. They're only a speck in space. Art should never have an owner. It's about an idea; and when people come to understand an idea, they own it."
>   **ANDREW ROGERS**, ARTIST, SCULPTOR OF GEOGLYPHS PHOTOGRAPHED FROM SATELLITES

"The thing I remember best about successful people I've met all through the years is their obvious delight in what they're doing, and it seems to have very little to do with worldly success. They just love what they're doing, and they love it in front of others."
        FRED MCFEELY ROGERS (1928-2003) EDUCATOR, MINISTER, SONGWRITER, AUTHOR, AND TELEVISION HOST OF PBS "MR. ROGERS' NEIGHBORHOOD, 1968-2001

"When you make music ninety-five percent of your life, it's good until it's gone. But I think it's emotionally very dangerous not to have other things you can be passionate about. I don't know what the future's about, but I can promise you it's going to be exciting."
        KENNY ROGERS, COUNTRY SINGER, ENTERTAINER, PHOTOGRAPHER, HOME DECORATOR, AT 67

Upon retirement after a 73-year writing career: "All this time I've been paid to say what is on my mind for television. You don't get any luckier in life than that. I wish I could do this forever. I'm not retiring. Writers don't retire, and I'll always be a writer."
        ANDY ROONEY (1919-2012) NEWSMAN, TV COMMENTATOR, WRITER, AT 92

"If you get a really short sense of time, then you have a really small sense of what's possible."
        ALEXANDER ROSE, DIRECTOR FILM DEDICATED TO LENGTHENING THE ATTENTION SPAN OF THE HUMAN RACE

"I want the audience to laugh, and then to go, 'Oh, I didn't know that.'"
        ISABELLA ROSSELLINI, ACTOR, WRITER, FILM MAKER, AT 58

"A lot of people don't end up happy. I'm interested in people when they're not happy. I began to write very bad, very sensitive stories, and I wrote these through college."
        PHILIP ROTH, AUTHOR, *PORTNOY'S COMPLAINT,* AND *I MARRIED A COMMUNIST,* AT 77

"I started taking pictures to record that world that I couldn't explain to people. I couldn't tell them what it was like being up on a rock, looking down, and looking around, what that adventure was like."
        GALEN ROWELL (1940-2002) NATURE PHOTOGRAPHER OF PLACES FEW PEOPLE COULD GO

"I said 'I'll just try comedy.' I would sit there (watching comics) and go, 'Why is this funny?' and 'Why isn't this funny?' After I wrote my first joke I was so excited; I called all my friends: 'I thought of a joke! I thought of a joke!'…. I like to take people away from the real world because the real world is a very complicated, upsetting place. I don't want to make anyone upset. I don't want to push the envelope. Let the envelope stay in the middle of the table. I'll just make you laugh."
    RITA RUDNER, COMEDIAN OF THE YEAR, AUTHOR, AT 54

"It was like being on a quiz show and they say, 'Do you want to take the money or see what's in the box?' I wanted to see what was in the box. But I waited ten years…. Maybe I didn't look the part, you know, 'you're not attractive enough'. But you have to ignore it; it's just gas."
    RUMER (SARAH JOYCE), BRITISH SINGER, AT 32

"Yes, I was afraid to take the role (Pink Panther). Sometimes it's good to be afraid."
    GOEFFREY RUSH, AUSTRALIAN ACTOR, FILM AND STAGE, AT 59

"A writer needs to internalize the work. Read aloud. Talk about it. Does this ring true? Is this my true voice? If you feel funny about reading aloud, there's something wrong with it — it's not your voice."
    JOANNA RUSS (1937-2011) SCIENCE FICTION WRITER

"Big Russ seemed to provide an invitation to people all across the country to talk about their dads."
    TIM RUSSERT (1950-2008) CNN TALK SHOW HOST, AUTHOR *BIG RUSS AND ME*

"I never wanted to be an artist… my background is from the theater. I want the objects out here to look like they're moving or dancing or performing."
    WILL RYMAN, ARTIST, SCULPTOR OF OUTDOOR INSTALLATIONS ON PARK AVENUE, NEW YORK CITY, AT 42

~S~

On Art Nouveau — 1890s-1914: "By the outbreak of World War I, it had lost its luster, but it left an indelible legacy. It broke forever all the bonds, all the rules and all the barriers that separated art and craft and

style. (Art Nouveau) was both an eruption of excessive fantasy and a scaling down to the minimal that announced the birth of the Modern Age.... It's a mistake to think modern art is about just rejecting the past; it's about repositioning the past. It's about deciding you're not in the past; it's available for you to use as you feel."
  MORLEY SAFER, NEWSMAN, ART COMMENTATOR

"When I was waiting tables in a café in Colorado, I wasn't a waitress; I was on my way to the Olympics. And so it makes every moment of your life better, no matter how hard your life is. If you're on your way to do something great, and even taking baby steps forward, you can feel better about each and every day because you know you're going somewhere better. People fall down; winners get up. But sometimes the gold medal winner is the person who can get up the fastest."
  BONNIE ST. JOHN, AUTHOR, *LIVE YOUR JOY*, MOTIVATIONAL SPEAKER, 1984 OLYMPIC SKIER WITH ONE LEG

"There is a marvelous peace in not publishing.... I like to write. I love to write. But I write just for myself and my own pleasure."
  J. D. SALINGER (1918-2010) AUTHOR, *THE CATCHER IN THE RYE*, AT 57

"For me to be a person who grew up in the '60s and still be center stage, I'm happy. I look for grooves in melodies. That to me is like the element is to conjuring a trance... taking them outside this doldrums existence into a place where they can also dream or aspire to touch their own light. When you touch your own light, you listen to the voice inside your own heart — the real you. One positive thought creates millions of positive vibrations. Those are the languages of light."
  CARLOS SANTANA, MUSICIAN; WOODSTOCK 1969, AT 58

(My 32-year marriage to Carlos) "is a perfect blend of emotion and wisdom. Simplicity. Soulfulness. Sincerity." (Carlos Santana's recipe for a good life.)
  DEBORAH SANTANA, AUTHOR *SPACE BETWEEN THE STARS*

Following a serious illness: "I thought, 'you have nothing to complain about. You have had a phenomenal adventure in life.' And I have."
  VIDAL SASSOON (1928-2012) BRITISH-BORN HAIR STYLIST OF THE 1960S, AT 83

"When women all over the world get together, to claim their rights — then whoo-ee! Then things will happen."
> JESSICA SAVITCH (1947-1983) NBC NEWS ANCHOR (ONE OF FIRST WOMEN TV ANCHORS)

"It's the flavor of my childhood. As soon as I see the pieces and hear the noise and touch them, it's this Pavlovian thing that's built in now. I've taken this toy that people are so familiar with, but made them think about it in a different way, almost make them forget that it is a toy."
> NATHAN SAWAYA, BRICK ARTIST, LEGO MASTER MODEL BUILDER, AT 37

"How do you tell a story in one image? How do you tell the whole story?"
> LAWRENCE SCHILLER, PHOTOGRAPHER, AUTHOR, *MARILYN AND ME*, AT 75

"I made the movie because I thought it needed to be made, and I didn't think anybody else could do it."
> JULIAN SCHNABEL, FILMMAKER, AUTHOR, INTERIOR DECORATOR, MOVIE DIRECTOR, "THE DIVING BELL AND THE BUTTERFLY", AT 56

"Anyone who works in a library knows that it's always the book next to the book you're looking for that is the very interesting one. It allows you to make those leaps of coincidence, imagination, happenstance, serendipity, that is the way we actually think."
> BEN SCHOTT, CURATOR OF KNOWLEDGE, INFORMATION ARCHITECT, *SCHOTT'S MISCELLANY 2008*, AT 33

"I find it (imitation by competitors) annoying, not flattering. You know why? An idea to me is like a child. If I bring anything to the table, it's that sort of sensitivity to what's in the air; it's not a logical thing, it's just instinctive. I trust my gut."
> IAN SCHRAGER, INNOVATIVE HOTEL DESIGNER/BUILDER, WITHOUT FORMAL TRAINING, AT 60

"I don't think I was called (to act). I was playing Nick Bottom in 'Midsummer Night's Dream', the jackass part. I was fifteen or sixteen and I made the donkey noise and I remember the audience laughing, and I went 'Ooh, that was cool!' I spent most of my childhood being

embarrassed. I think it made me an actor. You want to be somebody else. That's what I love about the theater. It's live. It'll never happen again. In the history of the universe, this event will never occur again."
    LIEV SCHRIEBER, ACTOR, STAGE, TV, FILM

"We were never in the coffee business serving people; we were in the people business serving coffee. I think at a time in America when people are hungry for human connection, we're providing that."
    HOWARD SCHULTZ, CEO STARBUCKS SINCE 1971, AT 57

"Wherever it can be shown, I'm open to trying, because right now we're at a time this great transformation is taking place in communication — the same way as the period of Georges Méliès (French pioneer illusionist and filmmaker)."
    MARTIN SCORSESE, FILM DIRECTOR, "HUGO", AT 69

"It is not my goal to be controversial.... I get up every day thinking, 'Let's be vanilla.' I don't think I've got to push a button today or create a headline or be controversial. I have no problem being considered *just there*. Vanilla goes with everything."
    RYAN SEACREST, RADIO/TV HOST, PRODUCER, VOICE ACTOR, AT 35

"Having a record debut on the Billboard Chart at No. 22 after thirty-some odd years... oh my god, I never thought that would happen. You know, I'm sixty-eight years old. This is a great thrill. Once you're at that Number 1 spot, you never forget that feeling. I'm still hoping."
    NEIL SEDAKA, SINGER, SONGWRITER, AT 68

"I love getting attention, like a child loves it, and it's never worn off."
    DAVID SEDARIS, HUMORIST, WRITER, PERFORMER, AT 54

"Some may find them merely diverting melodies. Others may find them incitements to Red revolution. And who will say if either or both is wrong? Not I.
At 90: (about his banjo) "This machine surrounds hate and forces it to surrender."
About writing songs: "I wanted something more peaceful."
From Emmy Lou Harris: "He's a living example of how you can change the world, one song at a time, one banjo tune at a time."
    PETE SEEGER, SINGER, SONGWRITER, PEACE ACTIVIST, ORIGINAL MEMBER THE WEAVERS, AT 53

"It was something like a bolt in the blue. It was so magic that it came to me and I wrote it in six weeks."
    ERICH SEGAL (1937-2010) AUTHOR, *LOVE STORY,* AT 33

"It's mysterious. You like to think you know what inspires you…, but I don't think you really do. It's great to look at a blank sheet of paper and walk up to an instrument and not know what's going to happen."
    BOB SEGER, ROCK MUSICIAN, AT 62

"Most actors are enormously talented and don't get as lucky as a few of us — and you'd better not ever forget that. I've hardly had a cross to bear. I mean, I've been very fortunate; I'm still working."
    TOM SELLECK, ACTOR, DIRECTOR, PRODUCER, TV AND MOVIES

"I pay no attention to anybody's praise or blame. I simply follow my own feelings. Mozart said it first, 'You have to follow your heart.'"
    BRIAN SELZER, MUSICIAN, "WOLFGANG'S BIG NIGHT OUT"

"Do parents sit down and tell their kids everything? I don't know. I've convinced myself — I hope I'm right — that children despair of you if you don't tell them the truth…. I feel like I'm working for myself at this point. If it's publishable, fine. If not, it makes not too much difference. Because I claim that this time is for me and me alone."
    MAURICE SENDAK (1928-2012) "KIDDIE-BOOK AUTHOR" (HIS WORDS), AT 83

"There's a wondrous magic to Christmas, and there's a special power reserved for little people, in the Twilight Zone."
From Charlie Osgood: "… not to mention the special power to see the world differently, reserved for Rod Serling alone."
    ROD SERLING (1924-1975) AUTHOR, DIRECTOR "THE TWILIGHT ZONE"

"The verb is one of the most powerful tools in a sculptor's toolbox. 'To live' is one such verb. Once I lifted the edge of a rectangular rubber mat and, in one action, created volume and contour (and a sculpture)."
On his sculpture "Supertankers": "It is supposed to be disorienting; think rational pure-form geometry based on optical illusion versus the emotionally disturbed geometry of mathematics."
    RICHARD SERRA, CREATOR OF LARGE OUTDOOR STEEL SCULPTURES (OPEN ENDED, STEEL WALLS WITH GEOMETRICAL CONFIGURATIONS TO CONFUSE), WRITER, SAILOR

— See **Note Bits on closing pages,** Creative Word Uses: "47 Verbs, How to Use Your Hands Artistically"

"It is important to maintain the courage of one's doubts as well as the courage of one's convictions."
　　Eric Sevareid (1912-1992) CBS newsman

"What I was looking for was to remember the times I had become a little bit more numb, when certain things happened to me in Vietnam. I was writing all the details of the stories, in lines, and the music started coming out. There was something that was circular, fading through the ear, that was helping me to choose what was the true part of the poem."

Ted's Poem For Tet (1995)
This is the poem that will save my life.
This the line that will cure me.
This word, this, the war word,
The one this breath,
The one I am.
　　Ted Sexauer, Vietnam veteran, poet

"Right after my first (piano) lesson, I started to figure out melodies myself, by ear. What I liked to do was play songs, figure 'em out, and play 'em. It was like unlocking some sort of a magical kingdom."
　　Paul Shaffer, musician, comedian, "Saturday Night Live" and "David Letterman Show", at 60

"I don't have any interest in politics. It's social justice really that interests me.... I have children. The only regret I have about having had four children is that I didn't have four more. Because that's how you know yourself — through your children."
　　Martin Sheen, actor in films, TV, at 71

"You have to write a lot of stuff to write something that's good. Write long; cut!"
　　Bill Sheff, comedy writer, novelist

"I say it in lots of different ways, but the message is: It's your life. Live it well."
　　Judith Sheindlin, TV's Judge Judy, at 69

"Nobody is just a typist, just a dishwasher, just a cook, just a porter, just a prostitute. Everyone has a story. Everyone here has at least one story that would stop your heart. Is this disjointed? Life doesn't have a topic sentence. There's nothing as clichéd as the story of a road traveled, of lessons learned, of obstacles overcome. But you know why? That's because it's the only story. It's the big story!"

  CLAUDIA SHER, ARTIST, ENTERTAINER, WRITER, PLAYWRIGHT, CREATIVE PERSON, "BLOWN SIDEWAYS THROUGH LIFE"

"News is very serious and I take the job very seriously, but I have tried not to take myself all that seriously. I think we all ought to take our hair down and have a little fun once in a while."
About his songwriting: I'm not giving up my day job, I guarantee you that, but I'm serious about it (music) like somebody who wants to be a really good golfer is serious about it. I love writing these songs. I know I'm never going to make it as a singer, but I might make it as a songwriter."
About political symbols: "I hope our national anthem will be sung one day in a hundred languages, and I am not worried about translating it, or that it will somehow dilute its message."

  BOB SHIEFFER, CBS NEWS COMMENTATOR, SONGWRITER, SINGER, BAND LEADER, AT 74

"What is most essential, most important in life, is invisible to the eye but not to the heart.... I lived in an old house. There was a legend that a treasure was buried in it somewhere, but no one was able to find the treasure. Perhaps no one even searched. But it cast a spell over the whole house.... Great expectations and no means to reach them. *Je crois aux actes et non aux grand mots.* (I believe in action and not in good words.)"

  STACY SHIFF, BIOGRAPHER OF ANTOINE DE SAINT-EXUPERY, AUTHOR, *THE LITTLE PRINCE*, AT 49

"Where did I get the idea? I saw the image of a woman awakened at three a.m., having a stranger at the door."

  ANITA SHREVE, AUTHOR, *THE PILOT'S WIFE*

"Without hope, I've been there. I didn't always have such confidence. And one day I just had to kinda sit down with myself and learn to really love myself, and be happy with myself, because I'm the only one whose opinion matters. I wake up with myself every day, and so I can't let anyone else diminish any confidence that I may have."

  GABOUREY "GABBY" SIDIBE, FILM ACTOR, "PRECIOUS", AT 26

"I decided that the best times I seemed to have were the moments I was onstage and I was determined not to let anybody interfere with those moments, not before the performance, not during the performance, and not after. When I look back on my life, I would rather say 'I shouldn't have done that' rather than 'I should have done that.'"
    BEVERLY SILLS (1929-2007) COLORATURA OPERA SINGER

"He (my father) thought it was hilarious to teach me dirty words, and I would say them, you know as a three-year-old, and get this wild laughter, you know, and it became addictive and it was like that kind of shock value, you know, became something that I was constantly seeking out."
    SARAH SILVERMAN, COMEDIAN

About Betty Buckley ("Cats"): "The really great singers — of whom there are not many — sing from the gut. That comes from a passionate deep inner self. That's the greatest kind of singing."
    JOHN SIMON, ENTERTAINMENT CRITIC

At 68: "Writing is peculiar — anti-social, somehow morbid. You disappear behind closed doors for years to talk to the ghosts in your machine. And then you want everybody to love what you've done. And everybody, meanwhile, has been feeling left out, parenthetical, and plagiarized."
At 79: "I find it easier to write in the way most of us talk. It just comes easier to me, and more realistic. It wasn't courage (to write a play); it was stupidity. You know you have to be so dumb and just say 'do it!' and maybe it'll work out."
    NEIL SIMON, AUTHOR, PLAYWRIGHT, "JAKE'S WOMEN"

"If I write a song and I really like that song, it's so great. It's like an ecstasy. I'm sure something's going on in my brain, that same chemical is flooding my brain, and my brain says, 'When are we going to do this again? Let's do this again.'"
    PAUL SIMON, SINGER, SONGWRITER, AT 64

"There's almost no reason for a human voice to be unheard on this planet now. That is an extraordinary thing. We're making the methods of communication accessible to almost everybody, and that's a great thing. I don't write books about things that are unimportant to me."
    SCOTT SIMON, NPR HOST, "WEEKEND EDITION/SATURDAY"

"These (photographs) are trying to show you a glimpse of creation."
    JONATHAN SINGER, PHOTOGRAPHER, SMITHSONIAN INSTITUTE OF NATURAL HISTORY

At 9 years old, Red told Ed Wynn: "That's what I'm going to do when I get older. I'm going to make people laugh."
Wynn: Ever see an audience before?
Red: No.
Wynn (holding the boy up to a peep hole in a stage curtain): Take a look.
Red: I fell in love with them (audience). That's my family; that's been my family all these years.... When the show's over, I walk into the empty auditorium and there's no applause, there's no echos of laughter, and I say to myself: "An hour ago I was important. Tomorrow I must start again." (from Dini Petty Show 1992)
    RED SKELTON (1913-1997) COMEDIAN, RADIO, MOVIES, TV, STAGE, AT 84

"We're writing for ourselves. If you're going to be a writer, you have to have a really thick skin because everyone is going to have an opinion about your material."
    MIKE SKULLY, WRITER "THE SIMPSONS"

"I just feel like I have this connection to oil paint that I can't let go of. And I don't feel very satisfied by anything else. The bell goes off and you feel like life is worthwhile and you've done what you were supposed to do."
    HUNT SLONEM, IMPRESSIONIST ARTIST, COLLECTOR

"What we learned from that night in this hall was that music becomes two things — it becomes a healing force and no matter what happens you can take down a physical structure, but you cannot take down the spirit of human beings, and that spirit is exemplified in their music. American music in the 21st Century parallels quite well English music."
    LEONARD SLOTKIN, SYMPHONY CONDUCTOR (AN AMERICAN CONDUCTOR AT ROYAL ALBERT HALL, LONDON)

"Take away taboo subjects — sex, appearance, money, religion — and what do you have left? Add the secret topics and you have drama! Surface may be dull, but underneath there are things that can't be talked about. But go on, talk about them. That is drama!"
    JANE SMILEY, AUTHOR, *THE GIFT OF IMAGINATION*

"I sit down; it's like going into a trance. I don't know what the process is. Subconscious is accessed in some way and out it comes."
>   **ALEXANDER MCCALL SMITH**, EDINBURGH, SCOTLAND
>   AUTHOR OF MYSTERIES, *THE NUMBER ONE LADIES' DETECTIVE AGENCY*

"There's a point where they (paintings) just come into sync. They feel done. They feel like they go with everything else, and then I stop."
>   **ALEXIS SMITH**, IMPRESSIONIST ARTIST, COLLECTOR

"This (success) isn't going to be here forever, this beautiful jewel, this shining diamond, is not going to be here forever. So while it's twinkling, what am I doing — personally, but also on a social level?
>   **ANNA DEAVERE SMITH**, ACTOR, PLAYWRIGHT, AT 61

"A writer has to keep himself interested. Writing is so boring, you're up there alone. Nobody's there. You sometimes swivel around to see if anybody showed up. No one ever shows up. If you aren't really fascinated by it (the story), it's not going to happen."
>   **MARTIN CRUZ SMITH**, AUTHOR *GORKY PARK*, AT 60

"You get ready to go on stage and your excitement builds and then it just explodes while you're out on stage, singing and dancing."
>   **R. J. SMITH**, MEMBER OF OLENTANGY KEYNOTES, HIGH SCHOOL SHOW CHOIR IN 2009, AT 17

At 59: "I wish you all could have met her (daughter Valerie Rose, 1975-2007). And I hope that in your lifetime you experience the exquisite *and divine love that I felt.*
At 60: Tonight and every night for the rest of my life, I will dedicate my show to my daughter Valerie Rose. 'I'm going to show you, Baby, that a woman can be tough."
>   **PHOEBE SNOW** (1950-2011) SINGER, SONGWRITER

On combating cancer: "This job is more fun than any job I'm ever going to have in my life; I love dealing with reporters. I love working with the President. And anybody will tell you that when you're trying to fight something like cancer, having good spirits, good attitudes, things you love doing, they make you better. I've got one of those jobs where I'm happy getting up in the morning. So I think it's good medicine too."
>   **TONY SNOW** (1955-2008) WHITE HOUSE PRESS SECRETARY 2006-2007, FOX NEWS ANCHOR, SYNDICATED COLUMNIST

"Is there a *formula* to give audiences what they like? If anybody could do that, they would be trillionaires. Every writer who has ever had a success wrote what they wanted to write. Nobody sits down and says, 'Now the formula for a hit show is a nun, a dog, and Abraham Lincoln.' It never works. Writing is about expressing the truth and saying, 'Look —isn't that interesting? Isn't she interesting? Maybe if you think about her, you'll think about yourself clearer.' All art is a form of education. It's not in my mind. Anyone who sits down to write a teaching show is likely to come up dry. I write shows because they're fun to write. Or better yet, so I can stand in the back of the theater and enjoy what I'm looking at.... I tend to write about the relationship between people, the relationships are what spark me. And plots. I love good plots."
    STEPHEN SONDHEIM, PLAYWRIGHT, STAGE PRODUCER

"I have a big problem with people who glamorize dumbness and demonize education and intellect.... I'm always the first actor to play the part; I'm playing it in my office as I'm writing it... it's a very physical thing. I'm talking out loud all the time, not just at my desk, but in my car. I start arguments with myself."
    AARON SORKIN, TV AND FILM WRITER/PRODUCER, AT 50

Song: "This Is How It Works:
    You're young until you're not.
    You live until you don't.
    You try until you can.
    You laugh until you cry."
"It's fun. It's a statement to yourself to be free. I have that very Russian Jewish thing of: tomorrow you might get a phone call about something wonderful, and you might get a phone call about something terrible."
    REGINA SPEKTOR, MUSICIAN, SONGWRITER, PIANIST, SINGER,
    AT 27

"I think escapism is needed and wanted. When that poor guy comes home from working that twelve hours a day and knows that he's having trouble paying his rent, I think they'd like to escape into a glamorous world — and I hope that's what we give them."
    AARON SPELLING (1923-2006) TELEVISION PRODUCER:
    "CHARLIE'S ANGELS", "FANTASY ISLAND", "DYNASTY"

"My work is really listening. Who was this person that we're going to remember? What did they love? What were they passionate about? How did they spend this short time on earth? Our soul is in this; our breath is in this; there are no two letters the same because they're drawn by hand. This is real. I think people are hungry for real."
    KAREN SPRAGUE, HAND CARVER OF TOMBSTONES

After twenty years of asking himself, "How can I hide something without burying it?" he found the answer: "I've got it!"
    MIKE STADTHER, COMPUTER PROGRAMMER "THE TREASURE TROVE" AND CREATOR OF PUZZLES IN CHILDREN'S BOOKS

"I was put here to sing. I was put here to spread the word. I will deliver you a song you will never forget. They'll have to scoop me off the stage. I will sing until I die."
    MAVIS STAPLES, GOSPEL SINGER OF R&B, AT 71

"My music combines feelings, music, God, spirituality, and prayer. I took something traditional, learned the rules, then broke them. Once you find yourself in a tradition, you can find your own language. Experiment with a number of different forms and traditions and styles. Tradition is the expression of commitment. One form of worship is through song. Pray to do it well, to move people, sometimes plaintively, sometimes with just the joy to be alive to play music!"
    ANDY STATMAN, MUSICIAN, JAZZ, KLEZMER, BLUEGRASS, "BETWEEN HEAVEN AND EARTH" ALBUM

"Wake up. You only live a short time. The unhappy ones are the people who let their parents talk them into doing something for a career that wasn't what they wanted – people who wanted to be writers or performers and decided to take the cautious route. (The happy people) made a decision to live, to do what their hearts told them, what's in them to do. Choose to live a life you want to live, not one that's safer or what someone thinks you should do."
    BEN STEIN, COMMENTATOR, ACTOR, WRITER, LAWYER, AT 65

"It takes a lot of time to be a genius; you have to sit around so much doing nothing, really doing nothing."
    GERTRUDE STEIN (1874-1946) WRITER, POET, ART COLLECTOR

"It's an accident... my career... I just kept on working and I never look too far ahead and I never look too far back.... I love standup comedians; I understand them. We all speak the same language. Standup comedians are like jazz musicians; they get each other."
    DAVID STEINBERG, STANDUP COMEDIAN, AUTHOR, DIRECTOR, HOST, AT 64

"Learn from the inside-out, rather than outside-in. Learning outside-in makes me feel like I should be like other people; learning inside-out makes me feel that I am good, I can give. This is my unique self. Force a lilac to be a petunia and you get a very angry lilac.... Women over 50 are like 10-year-olds — authentic, shit-free. When the gender roles are over, aging is like being a new country with no rules."
    GLORIA STEINEM, FEMINIST, AUTHOR, PUBLISHER, AT 71

"I tried every type of sport, every type of dance, and I never stuck with anything.... So when the acting came along, knowing that it is something a little more serious, that was my chance. I really wanted it."
    HALEY STEINFELD, FILM ACTOR, AT 14

"What happens to the subject when there is no object?"
    BARRY STEVENS (1902-1985) PSYCHOLOGIST, GESTALT THERAPIST

"For those people looking for Cat Stevens, you'll find him, you know, in this record ("Another Cup"). If you want to find Yusuf, go a bit deeper; you'll find him.... My voice is my trademark. It's me. I like the fact that if people hear my voice, they feel as if they know me, and that they can connect with me, and I think that's a gift. I want to just get heart-to-heart, make sure people understand some of the real, subtle beauties of what I've discovered."
    CAT STEVENS, SINGER, RE-NAMED YUSUF ISLAM (1979), AT 58

"One thing I learned in my most successful period is that before that I'd equated success and happiness as if they were the same thing. Well, they're not. You can be happy without being successful. My only ambition is to get better at what I do, better songwriter, a better singer, a better person. I would equate music for me as a kind of combination of two things: it's my mistress. It's also my religion. It's my spiritual link to creation; it's a spiritual path."
    STING (GORDON SUMNER) SINGER, MUSICIAN, MIXING STYLES OF COUNTRY, POP, JAZZ, AT 55

"Art is the tangible evidence of the ever-questing human spirit."
      MARILYN STOKSTAD, PROFESSOR OF ART HISTORY IN LAWRENCE KS, AUTHOR, *ART HISTORY*

"When you reach that age, you'd better have come to some conclusion that money isn't everything."
      OLIVER STONE, FILM DIRECTOR, AT 64

At 60: "That's what makes it (acting) worthwhile — the unexpected, the surprise, the extemporaneous. (Creativity) is like a spirit; as you approach an altar, part superstition, part belief, part… it is a gift…. Listening is everything. It's when you learn… everything. Listening to voices (from the past or those that may not have even lived) and sharing that voice with others."
About age: "Older women are terrifying, to everybody in the culture…. Our job now, ladies, is to put our heads down and hold our hands out and work like mad for all of our girls — to put their stories and their dreams on the screen where they're important, and to dispel the myth that it's a good fantasy."
About playing roles: There's a total immersion into the possibility — a life I could imagine I lived. That's infinitely interesting to me; there's no bottom to it. It's recognition of a like soul, something in there that I want to say…. We think there's a formula. Actually, the formula for happiness and success is being actually yourself, in the most vivid possible way you can, because then you don't have to pretend."
      MERYL STREEP, FILM ACTOR
      — SEE **MIKE NICHOLS**

At 67: "I'm very grateful that I still have one (voice) because I never exercise, sing. I'm more instinctive…. If I can identify as an actress to the lyric, and sail on the melody, it will be me."
On variety: "I do bore myself a lot. I have to go on… and it's not conquer… I don't know if I'd use the word conquer… it's expanding one's horizon. It's trying something new. It's risking failure. Even that's exciting to me. … I strive for excellence, but I don't think I'm a perfectionist. I have to compromise all the time."
At 69: "I don't even say that I'm retired. I think I could record for years to come, and direct movies and act in a few more. So, it ain't over till it's over."
      BARBRA STREISAND, SINGER, SONGWRITER, ACTOR, FILM DIRECTOR

"Big talent doesn't always win. People are scared to death of people who are really talented. I think I've got it — I know I've got it — and that's not to say anything. You know who gave me that, a gift of God to be given a great talent, and I've got it. Now it's up to me to handle it. And it's taken me a long time to get it right."
On being over 80: "You start to get older and one day you ask yourself, 'What's it all about, Alfie? What's going to happen? Do you love me? Really? Do I love you? Am I gonna die?' All the fears of a lifetime, and they've got no antidote. I've had that feeling you have to develop something in yourself to make you not afraid, something a helluva lot smarter and more powerful than you. If you get that, it's so uplifting. Something — God, faith. If I think I should win, I don't have to. I can't think of a better script than the one I've had, and the one I'm having, and the one I'm going to have."
    ELAINE STRITCH, ACTOR, "A DELICATE BALANCE" AT 82

"Put your heart and soul into it. Heart and soul!"
    J. C. STROBLE, ORDER TAKER, BEACON DINER, SPARTANBURG, SC, FOR 54 YEARS, AT 70

"People always say, 'How do you make it always look Anna Sui?' but it comes from my heart, like what it is that I love, and what it is that I'm excited about, and what it is that I want everybody else to know about."
    ANNA SUI, CLOTHES DESIGNER

"Fear and emotion can be addressed by reason only slowly, carefully, going back to the premise and trying to prove it. In open public debate — conflict, cultural opposition — minorities lose. We look to the government for leadership, yet how does government treat women? No E.R.A., no certification, treated like a minority. Sexuality, like religion, nationality and personal preference, is not visible. Gender, race, and physical appearance are obvious."
    ANDREW SULLIVAN, EDITOR, *THE NEW REPUBLIC*

"I was going to become a decorator. And after that, I thought, well you know, maybe I should just go sing. Because it's sorta easier. I've been a queen long enough. I'm older now; I'd like to change it and become an empress, okay?"
    DONNA SUMMER (1948-2012) QUEEN OF DISCO IN THE '70S, ARTIST, AT 59

GORDON SUMNER — SEE **STING**

"I can't think of any one point in my life when I've been happier, or had more fun. It's still hard work. Writing books is hard work, but when you're writing about something that fascinates you, it's a great, great deal of fun. I'm always laughing."
> **JAMES SWAIN**, MAGICIAN, AUTHOR OF MYSTERIES ABOUT CONVICTS AND GAMBLING (*FUNNY MONEY*), THE BOY WHO DREAMED OF BEING BOTH A MAGICIAN AND A WRITER WHO HIT THE JACKPOT IN ONE JOB

~T~

"Everything you do makes you loving. Do it with love. It's all about love."
> **ELIE TAHARI**, FASHION DESIGNER, AT 59

"I always thought my family was weird, too eccentrically weird that it would be unlike anybody else's experience. Not so! We are the same, for different reasons. Before you go out into the world, you must know the true story of your ancestors."
> **AMY TAN**, AUTHOR, AT 49

"If a bamboo artist keeps making the same things, people feel bored, and bamboo art will die out. But if I create something new, the world will realize bamboo can be used for different things."
> **SHOCHIKU TANABE**, BAMBOO ARTIST, FROM FAMILY OF BAMBOO ARTISTS, AT 36

"My work is kinda unmistakably me. I like that about it because I like me. (The characters) lead the way and I follow, and when they talk, I feel like a court reporter, just jotting it down…. It's really weird. When I'm writing, my vocabulary triples."
> **QUENTIN TARANTINO**, SCREENWRITER, FILM DIRECTOR, AT 46

"He has the joy! Now Benny Green is learning to juggle his affection and loyalty with what's been going on before, with his newly discovered need to create something of his very own."
> **BILLIE TAYLOR** (1921-2010) JAZZ PIANIST, COMPOSER, BROADCASTER, AND EDUCATOR

"You have to be ready to catch those things (inspiration) when they come down, you know, because they'll just fall right through and you'll forget them…. It is the most delightful thing that ever happens to me by far when I hear something coming out of my guitar and out of my mouth that wasn't there before… It's wonderful to live a life in music."
      JAMES TAYLOR, SINGER, SONGWRITER, AT 50

"Three events happen during a theater production: the performance, what is happening backstage, and what goes on in the audience."
About mask-making, puppetry, performance ritual, shadow plays: "Every artist can use a technique. Then you filter it through yourself, as an artist, and make it your own. We create a world. Are you with us? Then come on the boat and there we are."
On puppets: The first images on the walls of the cave came from women, as did shadows of a hand on the wall. So do origins of theater — puppets and masks."
      JULIE TAYMOR, DIRECTOR FOR THEATER, OPERA, FILM;
      DESIGNER OF PUPPETS AND MASKS; MUSICIAN, LYRICIST

"People will remember the conflicts. I wish they would forget them."
Q: Can you describe to a non-scientist what you find so joyful and rewarding about science, and physics specifically?
A: "No, just as little as I could describe my joy in listening to good music. I would find difficulty in describing (it)."
      EDWARD TELLER, PHYSICIST, WORKED ON THE ATOMIC BOMB

"The core of a successful trick is an interesting and beautiful idea that taps into something you would like to have happen… the deception is really secondary. The idea is first because the idea has to capture your imagination."
      RAYMOND JOSEPH TELLER, MAGICIAN PARTNER OF JILLETTE
      PENN (PENN AND TELLER), ILLUSIONIST, ACTOR, COMEDIAN

"Everybody has a story. What is the major story of your life, the one you've never revealed, one you keep re-telling, one that haunts you?"
From Charles Kuralt About Studs Terkel: "When Studs Terkel listens, everybody talks about old age and the Great Depression, about working, and race, about war and dreams."
From John Leonard About Studs Terkel: "What you get is courage. What you hear when these strangers talk is America singing."
      STUDS TERKEL (1912-2008) AUTHOR, AT 83

THE PLANETS, A SEVEN-MOVEMENT ORCHESTRAL SUITE, composed by Gustav Holst between 1914 and 1916 and included in the 1999 BBC miniseries, "The Planets". This magical space odyssey was performed in 2010 by the Houston Symphony Orchestra, conducted by **Hans Graf**, following the return of Astronaut **John Grunsfeld**, who carried his baton into space. British filmmaker **Duncan Cobb** combined film with concert for a spectacular production.

Astronaut Grunsfeld: "If you listen to Holst's 'The Planet' and close your eyes, you can imagine all kinds of far-out scenes. The real images are even better."

Conductor Graf: "Visually, with Saturn, you can't beat it. No human imagination could figure out such a beautiful thing."

Concert-goer: "The music brings it to life. You feel like you're there."

"If there was anything guaranteed in this industry, we'd be doing it over and over again.... The greatest thing that I've learned in my journey doing this is that if you come with your own agenda and your own ego, and try to force something and control something, you can't make a good movie."

        CHARLIZE THERON, FILM ACTOR, HUMANITARIAN WITH
        AFRICA OUTREACH PROJECT, AT 36

At 87: "What you look for, if you're interested in painting and drawing, are those things that captivate you in some way.... Along that line, his (Martin Ramirez, artist 1895-1963) work has this very riveting kind of attention. I think he had no idea he was making art. He just wanted to make these powerful images, which for him was a little kind of world. And those little worlds in painting and drawing are little human miracles."

At 91 (As pop artist, honored by the National Academy of Design in 2001): "I haven't the slightest idea what art is, but to be a painter is something which you have to prove... I have to confess. You are never really fully convinced of what you're doing. It's just part of the joy of it is what you keep hoping... I'd like them to laugh a little. If we don't have a sense of humor, we lack of a sense of perspective."

        WAYNE THIEBAUD, PAINTER, ARTIST

"Do not go gently into the night / While life is left to you / Make use of it / Do not just fade away."

        DYLAN THOMAS (1914-1953) WELSH POET AND WRITER

On being over 80: "I am a little more courageous in speaking out. Now I can express myself and go for broke. I've wanted to be a reporter from the time I saw my byline in a high school paper. My ego swelled and I was hooked for life."
    HELEN THOMAS, WHITE HOUSE CORRESPONDENT, AT 87

"Television's 'That Girl' was about a single career woman living alone at the beginning of the women's movement. I'm amazed that they still recognize me as 'That Girl'. It was a big wave and 'That Girl' just rode that wave. The mail we got was astounding; I took it very seriously."
    MARLO THOMAS, STAGE AND TV ACTOR, TV PRODUCER, WRITER, AT 66

"When you audition, you need the sense of pace, approach, and your need to get your nerves steady to know just where your strengths and weaknesses are. Everyone has to work at mastering this terrible focus of this little three-minute audition, which may shape your whole life."
    MICHAEL TILSON THOMAS, DIRECTOR, NEW WORLD SYMPHONY, AT 41

"This kind of work has the spirit of the craftsman. I put my heart and soul into it and whoever wears it can feel my spirit."
    KIHACHI TOBAI, KIMONO DESIGNER IN 200-YEAR-OLD FAMILY BUSINESS

"Art is the transfer of emotion from one person to another."
    LEO TOLSTOY (1828-1910) RUSSIAN AUTHOR, PHILOSOPHER

"What is the point of cashing in your chips? I'm going to do 'Hamlet' at 80."
    RIP TORN, ACTOR, "THE GOLDEN BOYS", AT 78
    —SEE **DAVID CARRADINE, BRUCE DERN**

"Art is like the soul of any culture. It's about being human, our search for why we're here. I thought I was going to die if I didn't keep working in the studio."
    MAYE TORRES, ARTIST, SCULPTOR, FROM TAOS, NEW MEXICO

"Folk music isn't just protest songs. It's love songs, it's children's songs, and it's songs about social issues."
    MARY TRAVERS (1937-2009) SINGER PETER PAUL AND MARY, AT 47

"Acting is a way of reflecting humanity and being part of life and lives that are not part of you."
JOHN TRAVOLTA, ACTOR, AT 53

"It's a good show; it satisfies one aspect of humanity that is very very important, and that is our need at a gut level to compete. We want to know how good we are, how fast we are."
ALEX TREBEK, TV GAME SHOW HOST; "JEOPARDY" SINCE 1984, AT 71

"I knew I wanted to write a story about a woman who had never been in love and who gave her life away, then one day looked in the mirror and said, 'Who am I?' The woman, the character, and the place: lonely, remote (remote doesn't mean cold; it means you gotta dig to get there) emotionally and in terms of traveling to get into this place (Big Stone Gap, Virginia)."
ADRIANA TRIGIANI, NOVELIST, TV WRITER, FILM DIRECTOR

"I have to be careful talking about this because you'll think me utterly mad. But I very much have a presence that I can't define that seems to be working when I write. You're talking to William Trogdon now. If you saw me writing a page of *River Horse* here a few months ago, you'd be talking to Heat Moon."
WILLIAM (LEAST HEAT MOON) TROGDON, AUTHOR, *WANDERLUST*, AND *RIVER HORSE*

"I don't do this just to make money. I don't do this just to have a certain level of fame. I do it because I want a challenge; I want to keep growing; I want to keep learning; I want to tell new stories; I want to find out something new about people and about myself."
STANLEY TUCCI, FILM ACTOR, WRITER, DIRECTOR, AT 49

"Why do artists draw in Paris? It's Paris! What more do you need?"
RICK TULKA, ARTIST, AUTHOR, *PARIS CAFÉ*

"(When I was 27) I was told I was too old for the music business. I was adopted, didn't look like anyone, my parents or my brothers. This gives you this sort of strange... kind of passport to not have to follow rules." *After singing at an outdoor Scottish Highlands Festival on her 32nd birthday:* "It's a funny thing. You're working on your birthday? It's like who told you this was work?"
K. T. TUNSTALL, SINGER, AT 32

"I lead a hyphenated life... I'm not sure that anybody is ever totally one thing. I have the freedom to follow my passion. That, to me, is what every person needs to find in their life.... There is nothing more dull and boring than a straight line."
  FATHER JEROME TUPA, BENEDICTINE MONK, PRIEST, ARTIST, FROM ST. JOHN'S ABBEY, COLLEGEVILLE, MINNESOTA, AT 62

"If I can get *U.S. Weekly* to cover global health, fantastic! Because it wouldn't be covered otherwise. And it's an extra bonus if you actually know what you're talking about."
  CHRISTY TURLINGTON-BURNS, MODEL, FILMMAKER, SOCIAL ACTIVIST, AT 42

On stage vs. film acting: "You have to push it as far as you can push it. That's my love. The stage is where I get to be as big as I can be — all my energy, all my size, all my voice. When I'm on camera, I feel a little too big. They're always saying, 'Bring your voice down a little, you know, energy down a little.' I always feel like I'm being sat on a little. But on stage, there is nothing stopping me. It feels great."
  KATHLEEN TURNER, ACTOR (MARTHA, IN THE FILM "WHO'S AFRAID OF VIRGINIA WOOLF?"), AT 51

"The difference between the almost right word and the right word is a really large matter. It's the difference between a lightning bug and the lightning.... I never write a book that doesn't write itself."
  MARK TWAIN (1863-1910) HUMORIST, AUTHOR
  —SEE **SAMUEL CLEMENS**

"I can't remember a time when I didn't envision playing the guitar, it being some sort of magical empowering thing. Passion would be a word, an obsession, a monomaniacal pursuit, not necessarily of technical prowess, but of warm music."
  JEFF TWEEDY, MUSICIAN, SONGWRITER, LEAD SINGER WILCO

"Sometimes the doors aren't opened that easy. Push hard enough and you'll force them open."
  ROLAND TYNAN, IRISH TENOR, DOCTOR, ATHLETE

~U~

On beginning his first stage role: "I'm just a firm believer; you gotta go for it and let the chips fall where they may. I'm nervous and I'm scared, and I've never been more excited in my life. The stage is where we get a chance, from the time the curtain goes up until the curtain comes down, to do what we do."
  BLAIR UNDERWOOD, ACTOR, PRODUCER, WRITER, AT 47

"Childhood is something of which only you are the pure custodian. There's nobody else around who knows. Returning, we find our snapshots inexact. Perhaps the condition of being alive is that the clothes, which in setting out we packed with love, no longer fit when we arrive. My attempt has been beyond a record of contemporary life, which is what you inevitably do; you try to make beautiful books — books that are in some way beautiful, that are models of how to use the language, models of honest feeling, models of care."
  JOHN UPDIKE (1932-2009) AUTHOR OF NOVELS, ESSAYS, POEMS, ON RETURNING HOME IN SHILLINGTON, PA

~V~

"The wide world over, cruelty is disguised as sport to gratify man's lust for excitement. From the early ages, humanity has congregated to watch the combating forces of man and beast."
  RUDOLPH VALENTINO, ACTOR, IN "BLOOD AND SAND", 1922 PARAMOUNT FILM

"You attract what you want. Your energy will attract it, and the phone will ring and your whole life can change in a blink."
  GLORIA VANDERBILT, HEIRESS, CELEBRITY

Quoting Zen: "What you see is what you see — nothing else."
  JAN WILLEM VAN DE WETERING (1931-2008) DUTCH AUTHOR, DETECTIVE MYSTERIES, NOVELS, *OUTSIDER IN AMSTERDAM*,

"When I discovered dancing (at 38), it was like flying. I thought, 'Where has this been all my life?'"
  DICK VAN DYKE, ACTOR, COMEDIAN, DANCER, ON STAGE, IN FILM AND TELEVISION, AT 85

"I feel a power within me to do something. I see my work holds out among other work."
    VINCENT VAN GOGH (1853-1890) DUTCH ARTIST
    — SEE **LARRY NICHOLS**

"I feel like I've been put on this planet to teach people to let their freak flags fly. I dress like a seven-year-old pirate from space. I give myself more permission than others to wear or do something different."
    KIRSTEN VANGSNESS, TELEVISION CHARACTER ACTOR, AT 38

From Morley Safer, CBS commentator: "The upstart intended to leave his mark on the world. And *that* he did, in full measure."
From Ronnie Bair, curator: "A superb genius who knows where to put every brush stroke, or every line, in the most economical way to achieve what he's after."
    REMBRANDT VAN RIHN (1606-1669) ARTIST

"I spent my whole life trying to learn about who I am. Being somebody else is a vacation. I like being second; I like being behind the scenes; I like being an advisor. I was born to do that. I don't know why."
    STEVEN VANZANDT (LITTLE STEVEN), MUSICIAN, ACTOR

"Fame is like a next door neighbor. Sometimes he waves and says hello, but you don't call him in the middle of the night if you're desperate."
    SUZANNE VEGA, SINGER, SONGWRITER ("LUKA" AND "TOM'S DINER"), AT 50

"The success of that dress taught me everything I know — about design, about women, about life.... I am as surprised of my success today as I was the first time around. But I'm not tired of it. I'm not tired of who I am. That would be sad."
    DIANE VON FURSTENBERG, FASHION DESIGNER, WRAP DRESS (1970), AT 64

"Tonight, write a six-line poem. Make it as good as you can make it. Then tear it up into six pieces and divide them among six waste baskets. And know that you already have benefited — by the creative experience." (TIAA Cref TV commercial)
On painting: I'm not an artist, but I often recommend it, that people practice art, no matter how badly; it's known to make a soul grow."
    KURT VONNEGUT (1922-2007) AUTHOR
    —SEE **DONALD FRIEDMAN**

~W~

"I try and follow my instinct about what I think they're (subjects) feeling and try lots of different ways to get them to show me those feelings in the photograph.... I have a feeling that I'll be taking photographs until the day I die. I know that's my desire."
  JOHN "RANKIN" WADDELL, LONDON PHOTOGRAPHER, AT 44

"Believe me, every day I say to myself I'm the luckiest man in the world, because I've had a great life at a wonderful career and a good marriage and wonderful children, and now I'm a grandfather. And you know, it's gone around and... I'm so aware of being fortunate."
  ROBERT WAGNER, ACTOR, MOVIES, TV, AT 76

"I had to leave (China) to grow. I wanted to learn something I don't understand. I want to create something I've never done before. I'm not trying to be East or West; I'm trying to make a bridge. It's part of who I am, my life."
From Charles Reinhart, director, American Dance Festival, and mentor:
"When I saw Chen Wai, the hair went up on the back of my neck, and it was one of those things that I knew what I was born for, which was to help the Chen Wais of the world."
  CHEN WAI, CHINESE-AMERICAN MODERN DANCER, CHOREOGRAPHER, AT 40

"To write a little three-minute song about a big event somehow makes you — me — feel like I'm in control of the situation. You're living alone! (Not really — he's in the same boat as all the rest of us.)"
  LOUDEN WAINWRIGHT III, COUNTRY SINGER

"I'm glad we persevered. I certainly hope that kids from all over the world will come to enjoy it."
  JANE WALENTAS, NY ARTIST WHO RESTORES CAROUSELS

"One has to continue to work to be as optimistic as one can. You can't butt against the wall and expect the wall to give way. You got to find a way of getting around it. More often than not, something unexpected happens — something that you could not have anticipated.... You don't want to be classified as an African American composer. Simply because we have worked so hard to be integrated as Americans."
  GEORGE WALKER, COMPOSER, FIRST BLACK TO RECEIVE A PULITZER MUSIC AWARD (1996)

At 71: "If you have a conviction, you have to stand your ground. And that's when the blood hits the floor. It really does."
At 93: "It's astonishing what you learn and see and feel along the way. That's why a reporter's job, you know, is such a job."
>   MIKE WALLACE (1918-2012) CBS NEWSMAN ON TV'S
>   "60 MINUTES"

"I want to work. I am going to be 95 years old, so I have to be careful. I have to keep my energy going, and I have to surprise people and have people say, 'Ooh, he's so old, but he's so nice.' That's what I do. I do it."
>   ELI WALLACH, ACTOR, MOVIES, TELEVISION, STAGE, AT 94

"This is what dreams are made of, people. Pursue your dreams. Never give up. Mine might seem strange, but anybody that's dealing with any battle, focus on that other side, and you'll achieve your goals, achieve your dreams.
>   NIK WALLENDA, HIGH-WIRE ARTIST, DAREDEVIL, THE FIRST TO
>   CROSS OVER NIAGARA FALLS ON A TIGHTROPE (TIME: 25:21),
>   ON MAY 16, 2012), AT 33

"I'm a dabbler; I'm doomed to be a jack-of-all-trades. And I thought, wait a minute — there's a profession for this. It's called acting."
>   KATE WALSH, ACTOR, AT 44

"I encourage others to reach for their dreams, strive for excellence, and do something they didn't think they could. If your dream doesn't work out, get a new dream."
>   DENNIS WALTERS, GOLFER, PERFORMER OF TRICK SHOTS
>   SITTING DOWN (IN HIS WHEELCHAIR), AT 59

"The music is what brought us together, but it's the people and the friendships and the relationships and the teamwork that keep us coming back."
>   HARRIET WALTERS, LEADER, LONG ISLAND GREATER NASSAU
>   CHORUS (WOMEN'S CHORAL GROUP)

"My parents didn't believe value and worth had anything to do with money. I think it's always been important to… keep your feet on the ground and your nose out of the air."
>   ALICE WALTON, WAL-MART HEIR, ART COLLECTOR, AT 62

Q: Why have you not created something new?
A: (cryptically) "Because it's easier to do."
Q: Why are you making these films?
A: "It's just easier to do. It's easy. The camera has a motor and you just turn it on and you walk away and it takes it all by itself."
Q: About your quote, "In the future, everyone will have fifteen minutes of fame", isn't this sort of a joke you're playing on the public?
A: "No! It gives me something to do."
               ANDY WARHOL (1928-1987) ARTIST

"I think it's nice to hang onto a bit of your childhood."
               CARL WARNER, BRITISH AUTHOR, PHOTOGRAPHER, FOOD ARTIST, AT 48

"If one thing lasts, I'm thrilled. I've made sixteen movies and if you like one of them, I'm happy. That's all you get sometimes. Most people don't get one thing that they're ever remembered for. That's why people have children. I make films."
               JOHN WATERS, FILM DIRECTOR AND PRODUCER, AT 61

"What I like to play is people in morally ambiguous situations. It isn't work; it's just long hours of fun.
               SAM WATERSTON, ACTOR OF STAGE, FILMS, TELEVISION, AT 69

"Living without color is like living without love. Everything is about color. The thing you remember is the color. Who doesn't want to be glamorous?"
               KELLY WEARSTLER, INTERIOR DESIGNER, AT 42

"I often work from the outside-in. I kind of meet the character in the middle somehow. Because I feel that it's part of the self expression of the human being."
               SIGOURNEY WEAVER, FILM ACTOR, AT 62

"I think it's how kids want to deal with artwork, hands on. I'm thinking of the house being a metaphor for how the mind works. In the kitchen, you make stuff. In the bedroom, you dream about things. In the living room, you experience them or view them."
               WILLIAM WEGMAN, PHOTOGRAPHER OF WEIMARANERS FOR VIDEOS, POSTCARDS, BOOKS, AT AN EXHIBIT CALLED "WINDOW INTO THE ARTIST'S EYE" AT THE CHILDREN'S MUSEUM OF MANHATTAN.

"I love you, and it's all I know."
>   **JIMMY WEBB,** SONGWRITER, AT 65

"If I could be 18 in 1963, I'd give it all up for that (following the drummer in your head). Life's too short to deny yourself things like this (attending Fantasy Camp) that make life much more colorful."
>   **JONATHAN WEISWASSER, MD,** VASCULAR SURGEON, TURNED DRUMMER AND PILOT, AT 43

"I've never been too trendy… I don't want to get too attached to the idea of it (success). I always like to keep myself in a state of slight anxiety, constantly aware of impending doom."
>   **FLORENCE WELCH,** BRITISH SINGER, AT 25

On writing well: "The gifts that come through me are special. Feel it! Feel it! It's in darkness that real growth takes place. You could die any day — all we have is this moment. You have to separate real from fictive to let the fictive develop."
On characters: "What she thinks of herself (whether she's trash, slut, or princess) depends on how she grew up."
>   **REBECCA WELLS,** AUTHOR, ACTOR, TEACHER

"When I was a kid, my grandma showed me a computer app that let me draw and write — I even wrote a book. Now, what I love to do more than anything is draw, doodle, paint, sketch, and I love to play with my characters. I like showing their images; they become real."
>   **KIONA WHEELEHAN,** ARTIST, WRITER, DOODLER, AT 19

At 89: "My secret? I learned it from my animal friends: kindness and consideration for somebody else. I think that keeps you feeling young."
At 90: "To be able to spend a lifetime in the business you love, with the people you love, and get away with it — it's just marvelous."
>   **BETTY WHITE,** ACTOR, COMEDIAN, FILMS AND TELEVISION

"You don't have to do the work to figure out what your life is. You feed your desires and your longings and they take you out into the world. They take you out, and you throw fuel on the fire. Your own life is just the moment your feet touch the ground. And you know it, only in the moment of contact. The soul would much rather fail at its own life than succeed at someone else's. Are you living your life? or someone else's?"
>   **DAVID WHYTE,** POET

After a teacher criticized him for writing small: "That made me *feel* small. She (my mother) said to me, 'You're now going to continue to make small things.' When I asked why, she said, 'If you keep making small things, your name will get bigger; the smaller your work, the bigger your name.'" (His first work was a sculpt of Charlie Chaplin on the tip of an eyelash.) "I haven't reached my peak; my work is still too big."
      WILLARD WIGAN, MICRO-SCULPTOR, ARTIST OF MINIATURES, AT 52

"When inspiration calls, you pick up the phone and you give it directions to your house. You don't mess around."
      WILL I AM (WILLIAM JAMES ADAMS JR.), SINGER WITH BLACK EYED PEAS, AT 34

"(The message from my father was) you're not quite as good as the rest, so you have to work harder. For a little kid, that stuck in my mind. We (the Williams Brothers) did work harder, and I did all my life."
      ANDY WILLIAMS, SINGER/ENTERTAINER, AT 81

"I began to understand the power of living on purpose. I'm a person who's found something that she's good at, and is doing it. I started acting in community theater, and the call keeps getting louder and I have to answer it."
      ANGELA WILLIAMS, ASPIRING ACTOR, WIFE, MOTHER, PASTOR, AT 30

"Right from the beginning, I chose tools that really worked. If you love what you do, then the world will fall in love with you. Well, I've been doing that for 94 years."
      CHUCK WILLIAMS, FOUNDER WILLIAMS-SONOMA COMPANY (HIGH-END COOKING UTENSILS), AUTHOR, AT 94

"I've always had a kind of vicious independent streak. A lot of the time I feel like I'm living hand-to-mouth, on people's compliments… There's just so much uncertainty when you're making your work, doing your job."
      MICHELLE WILLIAMS, ACTOR, FILMS, TELEVISION, AT 31

"I take it a little bit slower. I'm traveling at the speed of life right now. It's nice to say 'you have a great life. Just enjoy it. There's no rush.'"
      ROBIN WILLIAMS, ACTOR, COMEDIAN, AT 59

"There are probably more sacred things (than writing plays) you can do, but I cannot think of many. Continue to write and to have a belief in yourself that is larger than anyone's disbelief to do the best work you are capable of, and then push a little beyond that. Writing is living. To live life with dignity and to celebrate and to accept responsibility for one's presence in the world, and to leave to those who follow the gift of hope refreshed, is all that anyone can ask."
    AUGUST WILSON, PLAYWRIGHT

"You can't just be doing what you're supposed to do. It (interest in music in the 1970s) allowed me to step outside of the box. You're placed in a box naturally — I think most of us are. Listening to their music gave me an opportunity to see possibilities. Labels are stifling, unnecessary. It's a matter of not accepting the status quo, not accepting what everyone says you should be doing."
    CASSANDRA WILSON, SINGER/COMPOSER, THE JAZZ ORATORIO "BLOOD ON THE FIELDS" WITH WYNTON MARSALLIS AT LINCOLN CENTER

"With the kind of pictures they're making today, I'll stick with toilet paper."
    DICK WILSON (1916-2007) SPOKESMAN (MR. WHIPPLE) FOR CHARMIN ("PLEASE DON'T SQUEEZE THE CHARMIN"), AT 74

"I always wanted to sing; I always wanted to sing, but I didn't know how to do it. I didn't know how to make the singing thing happen."
    RITA WILSON, SINGER, ACTOR, AT 55

"I'm doing exactly what God wants me to do. When you're in your purpose, it shines. So I get lost in what I'm doing."
    CE CE WINANS, GOSPEL SINGER, GRAMMY WINNER, AT 45

"A setting can vary: hot/cold, water/dry/ time struggles, accidents, injustices, love affairs, unknown places we discover inside ourselves."
    OPRAH WINFREY, TELEVISION HOST; SHOW ON "WRITING AND WRITERS"

"I had an event where I think a lot of people have one in their life. Sometimes it's a crisis or a loss. Sometimes it's an accident, but something that just… it's a mortality sandwich and you have to eat it. I said, 'Ah, I better do what my deepest dreams are.'"
    DEBRA WINGER, ACTOR, AUTHOR, AT 53

"I like being me. I need to have normality. I really didn't want to be that famous (after 'Titanic'). I didn't know how I was supposed to deal with it. All of a sudden it wasn't easy to just go and buy a pint of milk and a newspaper. That was a half an hour ordeal that usually involved a bodyguard and 25 paparazzi. Literally, from one day to the next, it all changed completely; I was overwhelmed, really confused. I needed to know what it all meant and who I was."
  KATE WINSLET, ACTOR, OSCAR WINNER

About receiving acting awards: "I think I reflect life and I enjoy hearing that people enjoy me, because that's the real honor that you get."
  SHELLEY WINTERS (1921-2006) ACTOR, AUTHOR, AT 85

"The thing that very first started to drive me when I was 13 was a love of music, and I enjoy playing it, and I'm discovering more about music all the time. I just find it fascinating. Could I stop if I wanted to? I don't think so, no."
  STEVE WINWOOD, ROCK MUSICIAN, SINGER, COMPOSER, AT 60

"I have to switch on a switch consciously, to be able to do that (research). I just shut up and just listen."
On wearing white suits: "I realized I had a substitute for a personality, and still do. These white suits have been worth their weight in gold."
  TOM WOLFE, JOURNALIST, NOVELIST, AT 78

"This is the best. This is where theater to me begins."
  JOANNE WOODWARD, ACTOR, DIRECTOR, SMALL THEATER COMPANY OFF BROADWAY

"I've been accused of saying I was the greatest architect in the world, and if I had said so, I don't think it would be very arrogant."
  FRANK LLOYD WRIGHT (1869-1959) ARCHITECT

"Art has never been something that I have been able to just throw on the back burner. I've found this time in my life when I haven't had time to do art. I go crazy. I felt that I was unable to do the rest of my life. I have to be creating."
  JANIS WUNDERLICH, ARTIST, SCULPTOR, AT 38

On his 80th birthday: "I just want to get to the truth of the thing. You can't pussyfoot! Just ask. You have to believe in what you do! ... I have my own world, over in the corner, watching, not a part of the world, an

observer. To see without being there, just a pair of eyes. I want the picture to be personality — not me. When you know something and feel it and have a love for it, my god, do it. Don't let it go by! It's all in here. It's what you take to the object that counts. My world is getting smaller and smaller... and bigger and bigger.... I paint what I want to paint: feathers, clamshells, a real thing. I don't paint to be free, like abstracts, but objects that don't have any story to them at all — just color and shapes. The less you have in a subject, the better the picture." *About painting nudes*: "I don't think it's that (shock). I just want to get to the truth of the thing. I like to see a thing clear, and I'm not ashamed of it at all. You've got to believe in what you do."
  ANDREW WYETH (1917-2009) ARTIST, PAINTER

~Y~

"Bubble making is not just an art, but a science. I enjoy it because the memory of the moment stays forever. Bubble is beautiful to watch. It is very eye catching, visual, but it has an independent life. I'm always thinking of making something new because, I have to say, there is no boundary now but the imagination. You can create the moon, the stars, the sun."
  FAN YANG, BUBBLIST
  — SEE **GOEFFREY AKINS**

"I was very naïve. I thought that you will be discovered. No matter what you do, people will find out about you. Well, 15 years later, nobody really cares. (After six years of being out there) I'd overdone it. I went too far. I took time off, wrote a book, and learned to pace myself."
  YANNI (YIANNIS HRYSOMALLIS), GREEK MUSICIAN

"I was very stubborn and I thought, yeah, you can have it all; you can do it all. And I'm not sure you *can* do it all. Music was really it for me. It still is. I think now if I'm ever in a relationship again, it will have a place that is more proper. It can still be important, it can still be who I am, because it can define who I am for sure, but it can maybe have its proper place."
  TRISHA YEARWOOD, SINGER/SONGWRITER

"Once women anywhere discover what it feels like to be independent, they're hooked for life. It's like in America. It's very powerful. I can decide what I want."
    XIAO HUA YU, OWNER, LUCKY BAG COMPANY, CHENGDU, CHINA, AT 24

~Z~

"I like to make entertaining pictures, but you can make entertaining pictures that have just a seed of something that people benefit from, that aren't mindless. It's not just entertainment."
    RICHARD ZANUCK, FILM PRODUCER, AT 77

"You touch them (pottery pieces); you use them; yes, they are comfortable. There are no hostile pieces. (My work) is a playful search for beauty. First of all, they (the pieces) should be useful, then beautiful. Because what good is a beautiful piece that you can't use?"
    EVA ZEISEL, (1906-2011) BUDAPEST POTTERY ARTIST, AT 98

"I just thought, 'Why not? What is there to lose?' First it was a little overwhelming, almost like a puzzle, being able to decode something. I think it was more of a 'this is really cool; I wonder if it works' sort of thing. It was pretty amazing. I'm excited to learn everything in the sciences… even computer science, making new innovation possible."
    ANGELA ZHANG, HIGH SCHOOL STUDENT WHO DISCOVERED POTENTIAL CURE FOR CANCER, AT 17

NOTE BITS ESPECIALLY FOR WRITERS

Among my notes, as I put together this book, I found the following slips of paper — among others. They tell the story of "Singing Your Song" rather well. They reflect the yearning, the frustration, the courage to jump off a ledge and become something new and never-before-seen.

What follows are notes that I found important to keep. I print them as part of my therapy to move my brain from left to right. If you're stuck in your left brain, close your eyes, take a deep breath — a very deep breath — and absorb some of these words. (Keep the left side of the brain closed and sleeping while the right side plays!)

You may discover a sense of dreaming, that all-consuming activity that we all experience.

Creativity is...
...taking what you know and using it in expanded ways.
...coming up with new ideas, new products.
...the ability to be insightful and to provide original solutions.
...becoming a pioneer in many aspects.
...a wealth of experience that enables one to see beyond the obvious.
...an enormous reservoir of background, knowledge, and experience.
...wisdom.
...insight.

General Comments from the Lakewood Writers Group:
"The worst part is what drives me; the best part makes me want to sing."
"It's only too late if you don't start now."
"After 60 there are no rules!"
"Do what you want — until you're told not to."
"Find what you love — and do it! Over and over again!"

Inside the Actor's Studio, TV show for nearly 20 years:
As James Lipton asks his guest Originals, ask yourself: "If you weren't doing what you're doing, how would you choose to spend your time?"

From **Okeelah and the Bee**, *book and movie:*
>Our deepest fear is not that we are inadequate
>Our deepest fear is that we are powerful beyond measure.
>We ask ourselves, who am I to be brilliant, gorgeous, talented, and fabulous?
>Actually, who are you not to be...?
>We were born to make manifest the glory of God that is within us,
>And we let our own light shine.
>We unconsciously give other people permission to do the same."

Songs Pete Seeger made famous:
>*This Land is My Land* (composed by Woody Guthrie, sung at inauguration of President Barach Obama)
>*If I Had a Hammer*
>*Where Have All the Flowers Gone?*
>*Turn, Turn, Turn*
>*Michael, Row Your Boat Ashore*
>*Tsena Tsena Tsena*
>*Goodnight Irene*
>*We Shall Overcome*
>*So Long, It's Been Good To Know You*

God is a Woman! Here's proof:
Thank goodness God put our eyes where we can't see the wrinkles! See, I knew God is a woman. I'd love to get my hands on the dope that invented the mirror. If we couldn't see the wrinkles, we wouldn't know they were there.

Three Guidelines for Writers

Writers are always looking for approval, acknowledgment, sanction: "Tell me it's good." I have three rules for writers:

1) Do not listen to critics (good or bad)
2) Never Never Never show a draft before it's ready
3) Trust yourself and write your way.

The Internet:
If all the ideas of all the people in the world were laid out end to end, we'd have... the Internet!

Definition:
A Freudian slip is when you say one thing and mean a mother." (Anonymous)

How Metrics Changes Our Language
    Instead of: Give 'em an *inch* and they take a *mile*
    You'll say: Give 'em a *centimeter* and they take a *meter*
    Go the extra *mile* .... Go the extra *meter*
    Best foot forward .... Best *third of a meter* forward
    Won't give an *inch* .... Won't give a *centimeter*
    *Yard*arm .... *Meter*arm
    Inch along .... *Centimeter* along
    Walk a *mile* in my shoes .... Walk a *meter* in my shoes
    Foot-long hotdogs .... *Twelve centimeter*-long hotdogs

Punctuation Challenge
"Want something you can't have — it's something to live for."
[*Where you place a question mark, comma, semi-colon, or exclamation point in that sentence will tell you much about yourself.*]

Yearnings and Characters
Make your characters restless, bad citizens, bad spouses, bad children. Inject a moral and religious search of humanity and sex. Sex is the means whereby the search is conducted. It is ecstasy, transcendence of oneself. Sexual and spiritual greed are closely allied. As a writer you can reconstruct yourself. (Writers: re-read the above slowly and digest completely.)

From a Readerboard
    Shut up
        Pay Attention
            Ask Questions
                Keep Trying

The Great Depression: October 29, 1929.
The Great Depression was on its way. Not a person in the country was not affected by the shattering of hope. [*Is it any wonder with all those negatives and double negatives in that sentence?*]

Creative Word Uses
47 Verbs, How To Use Your Hands Artistically

Richard Serra lists 47 verbs of things an artist can do with hands to make art. Ready? Here they are:
Roll, bend, grasp, fold, fire, split, tear, cut, twist (torque), enclose, surround, encircle, modulate, distill, smooth, pinch, twirl, punch, knead, scoop, smear, push, pat, hit, slap, press, tap, clench, squeeze, shake, pluck, scratch, snap, break, tie, lace, braid, pull, sift, scrape, gather, stretch, compress, pile, stack, salvage, store, rescue. (Okay, you got me — that's 48!)

Order Blank

Are You Singing Your Song?

Use this convenient form to order additional copies:

Please Print:

Name _____

Address _____

City _____ **State** ___ **Zip Code** _____

Phone _____ **Email Address** _____

    _____ copies of book @ $16.95 each   _____
(WA residents add $1.53 sales tax)   _____
Postage & Handling @ $4.52 per book   _____

    Total Amount Enclosed   _____

Check / money order payable to: **Muddy Puddle Press**.
Mail to: Muddy Puddle Press
             PO Box 97124
             Lakewood WA 98497

Visit **www.valdumond.com** to place your order quickly and securely through PayPal.

Email other inquiries to: muddypuddle@live.com
View Val's books at www.Amazon.com/Author

Made in the USA
Lexington, KY
06 August 2012